# Marrying Up

## An American Dream— and Reality

# Marrying Up

## An American Dream— and Reality

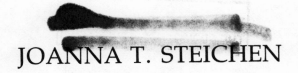

## JOANNA T. STEICHEN

**RAWSON ASSOCIATES:** *New York*

Library of Congress Cataloging in Publication Data

Steichen, Joanna T.
  Marrying up.

  1. Marriage—United States. 2. Social mobility—United States. I. Title.
HQ536.S73   1983        306.8'1'0973        82-42696
ISBN 0-89256-231-5

Published simultaneously in Canada by McClelland and Stewart Ltd.
Composition by
Westchester Book Composition Inc.
Yorktown Heights, New York
Printed and bound by
Fairfield Graphics
Fairfield, Pennsylvania
Designed by Jacques Chazaud
First Edition

*To the memories of Bunby, W. J. T.,*
*and the perpetual motion machine*

# Contents

# Acknowledgments

Jeffrey Hollender and the Network for Learning provided the framework in which much of the material in this book first confronted the varied expectations of a sizable public.

Eleanor Rawson contributed her quick and sensitive grasp and her illuminating style as an editor. Julian Bach supplied kindness and grit as my agent.

Encouragement and helpful suggestions at many stages of this project flowed liberally from Hyman Spotnitz, Joan Daly, Edward Albee, Skip Rozin, Lucille Schulberg Warner, Doris O'Donnell, Sebastian Walker, Olga Hirshhorn, Dan Meyers, Jonathan Thomas and the late Aaron Stein.

Cheerful assistance on a challenging schedule came from Julie Guibord Rozin and Edna Taub, who did research, Glyn O'Malley, who coped resourcefully with human curiosity and mechanical things, Jane Woolman, who freed me from the administrative desk, and Gary Waber and George Dispigno, the most expeditious of photocopiers.

Many friends and acquaintances volunteered anecdotes and offered examples. My patients and my true colleagues learned to tolerate the public side of my life.

All of them have my admiration and gratitude.

J. T. S.

# Before You Begin

This book may make you angry. Its subject is a universal fantasy, acceptable in public as a joke about other people—taboo as an acknowledged personal goal. This book takes that fantasy out of the closet and examines how it works in reality. It decodes some euphemisms and unmasks some polite hypocricies that people use to disguise their motives. Though it does not recommend in choosing a mate that the top priority go to money or its equivalents in status and power, it does advise that the potential effects of a spouse's particular financial or social position be faced squarely. It also offers some examples and guidelines for men and women who want to include marriage in their plans for upward mobility. But it offers no magic, no simple key to the one place to go to meet the perfect rich single for you. Its suggestions call for work, discipline, risk, and sacrifice. Some of these ideas may turn out to be things you already knew and didn't want to face in the first place.

The book began as a course I taught for New York's Network for Learning, starting in September 1981. Before then, my teaching was clinical: I helped other psychotherapists, individually and in groups, to develop some of the skills they needed to work with patients. (A psychotherapy patient can be anyone who is baffled by a set of life circumstances or is stuck in patterns of self-defeating behavior and wants to change.)

From the moment the Network for Learning announced my *How to Marry Money* course, there was a contagious clamor of response. I spent most of a week's vacation on the telephone doing interviews with newspaper and radio journalists all over the United States, as well as in England and Australia. *The Wall Street Journal* ran an article. A London newspaper sent a reporter and a photographer out to my summer cottage by seaplane. There were appearances on the "Today Show," the "Phil Donahue Show," "PM Magazine," Showtime Cable TV and many local TV and radio programs. Magazines, among them, *US, Vogue, The Saturday Evening Post*—even Japanese *Cosmopolitan*—ran stories about the course.

On TV and radio call-in programs, some of the audiences were defensive. The wives of factory workers thought they were being told they had been stupid not to marry for money. Middle-aged women with affluent husbands feared their daughters would be courted only for their money. A young multimillionaire believed women only wanted his money, but he never had considered giving up the Porsche and other symbols of wealth that made his status obvious. A pattern developed. After the programs went off the air, the members of the audience who really wanted to know how to go about marrying money would come up and start asking their questions. Letters came in from all over the country. Some writers were cocky and scornful of the hometown pickings; some sounded sad and desperate. Everyone wanted to know more.

Among my own acquaintances, the reactions fell into distinct categories. Those who were self-made rich and proud of it said, "Great! I'll take the course. You can never have too much of a good thing!" Those who had inherited wealth and married poorer people were wary. Would I embarrass them? Would I shake their faith in their own spouses' motives? Why was I going public with things "everybody knew" but wasn't supposed to talk about in socioeconomically mixed company? Some people expressed distaste, found the subject "tacky." They usually turned out to have been raised by upwardly striving parents who wanted their children to fit in with higher class people and had taught them, most *un*aristocratically, that it wasn't nice to think about money. A few people, those whose dirty little secret had been the relentless pursuit of wealth as the primary qualification in a spouse, stopped speaking to me.

The *How to Marry Money* classes were given once or twice a month for a year in New York City and are still repeated from time to time. The number of students was as high as 150 in one class. Who came? To say everybody seems only a slight exaggeration. Ages ranged from the late teens into the sixties. About a quarter of the students in each class were men. Some of the students were divorced, some widowed, and some were still married. Some were sent, they said, by their mothers or fathers. Most ethnic groups were represented. Students came from all over the country. Some scheduled vacations in New York City around the class date. Even some of my friends who had married money and were wondering what to do next came to the class. Colleagues attended to see if they could offer some version of their own. And imitations began springing up in several cities.

The students represented a great range of occupations: all the professions, most of the creative and performing arts, everything from the lowest echelons of the service occupations to the upper echelons of business. There were some people who didn't work and didn't have to, some who were marginally self-supporting, at least one bona fide gigolo, and a self-proclaimed "stud" who, for a price, married rich foreign women seeking permanent residence in the United States.

Some of the students announced that they were already rich. They were "simply curious," checking out the enemy's strategies, wanting to know how they compared to the rest of the world, or wanting to see if they, too, could broaden their choices and move up through marriage. Some students were bitter; they came to use the class, as they probably did most other experiences, as a self-fulfilling prophecy to prove that life was a cheat and there was nothing out there for them. Their participation was confined to offering reasons why each suggestion could not possibly work.

Several pretty young women reported that they met plenty of rich men, but these were all boring. They wanted to know how to find the interesting ones. Successful young executives of both sexes complained that they wanted equally prosperous mates but could not find any who were also kind, attentive, devoted and generous. Then there were the "show me" girls. They came in pairs, always late, rattling packages, talking nonstop to each other, usually dressed in some fantasy of tough chic. They just wanted to know the names of the places to go, the bars where the rich singles hung out.

Several students wanted to meet billionaires. Others had quite modest financial goals. Some were primarily interested in characteristics that had more to do with class, culture and education than with gross assets, net financial worth or earning power. A few were interested *only* in money; an orangutang with enough of it would do. Many cared more about character and compatibility and wondered if love could be combined with money. It became clear that "money" meant many different things. Very often the fantasy of marrying "money" didn't refer to money at all but to certain images of breeding, achievement, clout in the community or personal style. All of these represented ways of moving up in the world.

The students who wanted a complete blueprint, like the

feet painted on the floor to learn the dance steps, tended to be disappointed. Some students didn't want to consider changing anything about themselves or doing any extra work to attract a richer spouse; they tended to get angry and stalk out early. But others reported that the class reminded them of resources in their present lives that they had overlooked. Many made note of suggestions about career shifts, changes of location, and development of new interests or attitudes. These were things they could use as starting points for themselves.

Still other students said the class raised serious questions about their self-esteem and the choices they made, and they would like to get more help in answering these questions before deciding which goals to pursue. Others felt the class helped them to consider more realistically the many issues involved in marriage. Some reported it made them realize they didn't care that much about money or moving up, after all. And others decided they wanted to concentrate on achieving success on their own, independently of marriage.

All the issues discussed in the *How to Marry Money* class, and a lot more, are in this book. You can read it in order to compare it with your perception of how things work in the world or to decide on a course that makes sense for you, individually. The available realities may not offer the boundless splendor of your most extravagant daydreams, but marrying up to money, power or social position is like any other goal. Its specific fulfillment varies somewhat for men and women, for young people and older ones, for first marriages and later marriages. The brilliant, the average, the plain, the beautiful, those who start poor and those who start rich, cannot expect to attract the same mates. Occasionally, without even trying, someone stumbles into upward mobility through accident or luck. But luck and accident can't be taught, while how to work toward a goal is something any willing person can learn.

Be careful how you answer this question: Would you really want to marry up? You may have more choices than you think.

J.T.S.

# Part I

---

# Goals

## The choice to marry up

It is a truth universally acknowledged, that a single man in possession of a good fortune, must be in want of a wife.

However little known the feelings or views of such a man may be on his first entering a neighborhood, this truth is so well fixed in the minds of the surrounding families, that he is considered as the rightful property of one or other of their daughters.

Jane Austen
*Pride and Prejudice*

# *1*

---

# *Double*
# *Standards*

### *Breezy Samantha*

Samantha sparkles with gentle high spirits and classic good looks. She drives the old Ferrari that is left at the country house. She does not cook. She never wears her Bulgari bracelet to her job in geriatric rehabilitation, but everyone at the hospital knows she is rich. There are so many clues: the cut and variety of her clothes, the not quite concealed little weekends in London or Barbados or Aspen, the food stores to which she telephones orders, the magazine article showing the sculpted, open interiors of her turn-of-the-century carriage house, the honorary commissions on which her charming and distinguished husband serves. Her colleagues suspect she has little affairs on the side. Her father, who was supposed to have adored her, was a businessman without an office, spinning out his schemes at the track or the bar, sometimes flush and with a woman on his arm, sometimes with nothing but a song and dance for his creditors. Her mother lived for a time on welfare.

Ever since she was seventeen, Samantha has earned a

decent living at various respectable jobs requiring nerve and quick judgment in cities on both coasts and in Paris. She knows she can do it again. In fact, she is still working, now developing an innovative geriatric care program with the modest professional credentials of a social work degree. She never has been without a man, but only two or three have mattered much. Greg, her husband, is one of those. He is eighteen years older than she is and an inch shorter. His charm emanates from a confident personality rather than excellent bone structure or symmetrical features. She admires his flair, his imagination, his pragmatic way of trading off a certain amount of public-spirited ideals for a certain amount of good business practice. She is capable of leaving him if he does not treat her well, but she would prefer to stay. They appreciate each other. She'll be forty soon. Excitement and variety still matter to her, but now she thinks about the future. And while she never has craved luxury, she wears it so well.

Samantha married money and position. She considers it accidental, and she doesn't mind admitting it in a softly astonished way. Actually, it is unlikely that she would have married and stayed with a poor or undistinguished man. She is a person of outstanding style. She is pretty, energetic and outgoing. She commands respect. She is willing to work and pay her dues, but she has no driving career ambitions of her own. A streak of common sense underlies even her most madcap choices. To be worthy of her a man has to be bright, competent, daring and at home in the world. Unless they are extremely self-destructive, such men usually obtain some portion of the material goods and honors the world has to offer.

## Diligent Daphne

Daphne's course was more deliberate. Her family was white collar working poor, though they liked to think of themselves as shabby gentility. Daphne was their obedient hope. Her mother stayed up all night sewing frilly dresses for Daphne to wear to Friday afternoon dancing class. Daphne loved the piano and had considerable talent. The earnings from a musical career would have been too uncertain, however, and the demands of preparing for one would not have left time for the family's important goals. Daphne's capacity for discipline was applied in other directions.

She smiled sweetly through scholarship teas where the socially deserving (though not necessarily the most intellectually promising) girls were selected for the nice private schools and colleges. She made friends with rich girls and never dated a Catholic or a boy from the public high school. She stayed in a nice college long enough to qualify as an alumna and come a little too close to scandal with her socially prominent roommate's handsome brother, Christopher. Then she took a job at a nearby university, a clerical job carefully chosen for its exposure to bright, ambitious young men engaged in prestigious professional training. After rigorous screening and some sampling of prospective candidates, she settled on Philip and concentrated on getting him to marry her.

Philip was completing his training near the top of his class. Though not rich, his family was more solidly middle class than Daphne's. He was physically awkward and in no way handsome, at a loss for general conversation and, at first, a bumbling clod in any kind of sexual encounter. But he was smart, hard-working and reliable. He hadn't been planning to marry right out of school. It had occurred to him that it might be worth his while to wait and look over the daughters of the prominent families in the community where he would establish himself professionally before thinking about a wife. However, Daphne set about making herself indispensable. She typed his reports and ironed his shirts, gave him back rubs and remembered his parents' anniversary. How had he ever managed without her?

Phil's professional skills were at a premium in the growing community in which they settled. Daphne was eager to
demonstrate the domestic and social virtues of a respected
professional man's wife. They were rewarded soon enough
with money and a basis for social position. Daphne is now
sometimes referred to as one of the community's cultural
leaders. Her most restful leisure-time activity is supervising
the flower arrangements for the church (Episcopal) on alter-
nate Sundays. She is on the board of the local symphony.
(She maintains a properly maternal interest in the young first
violinist who left to pursue a conducting career abroad, and
she may not even realize that she was in love with him for
a while.) Her new living room seats forty comfortably for
chamber music recitals. The family room mantel is lined with
her daughter's horse show ribbons and her son's tennis tro-
phies. A catamaran and a sailfish as well as a speedboat are
kept at the lakeside cottage. Daphne and Phil have been to
most of the major European music festivals. Every three years,
instead of trading it in, Daphne gives her old station wagon
to her parents. As is customary in her community, she has
only part-time household help and does all of her own cooking, although most of Daphne and Phil's serious entertaining
is done at the country club, anyway.

Daphne considers her life satisfactory, successful and well-
deserved. She has tried to imbue her children with decent
values and teach them not to take their good fortune for
granted. They are beginning to leave for college now. She
hopes that their lives will never be warped by some inap-
propriate, searing passion.

In one of our society's most traditional ways, with fore-
sight and discipline that began in childhood, Daphne married
up by choosing a man with obviously superior career prospects. But Daphne will not discuss the subject. It is her dirty
little secret. The approved version of the story is that she and
Phil just happened to meet in the Dean's office and fall in

love while he was completing his training and she was working at the university because she liked the cultural environment so much. To admit that, at nineteen, she chose the location of her job with a particular kind of marriage prospect carefully in mind and that her affection for Phil was a deliberately acquired taste rather than an instant thunderbolt would somehow put her morality in question. To satisfy her sense of propriety, Daphne has to deny a large portion of her own competence and determination, qualities that in other circumstances she could acknowledge as admirable.

If Daphne and Samantha were to meet, Samantha would probably find Daphne's manner cloying. Daphne's affluent world has a thoroughly middle-class orientation. Conventional appearances are important in all aspects of life. Traditions are self-conscious. Humor is strained. Samantha is at home in more cosmopolitan and upper-class circles, a combination of cultured background with refreshing infusions of new money. Wit and originality are valued, and the skeletons occasionally poke rather carelessly out of the family closet. In Daphne's world, someone with artistic leanings might call the dog Picasso, or maybe Pablo. Samantha's Abyssinian cat is called Ruiz. At a meeting between these two successful women, Daphne would circle warily around the breezy Samantha and dismiss her later, to friends or to Phil, as an adventuress who obviously had married for money.

## Mother's Milk and Sour Grapes

Clearly, marrying up (which most often means marrying money) is a subject that elicits nervous laughter and mean suspicion. Some of this comes from barely concealed envy of another's apparently effortless success in a society that still pays lip service to the value of hard work. But money can be "dirty" in so many ways. When someone else does it, mar-

8    MARRYING UP

rying money is often seen as marrying *for* money. Marrying *for* money implies that nothing else about the person matters, only the money. Since marriage usually includes some kind of sexual activity, and in most people's minds sex for money without love equals prostitution, the embarrassment and the need to register disapproval come from the uneasy impression that marrying money sounds uncomfortably like prostitution.

So why would someone whose professional career as a psychotherapist depends on maintaining a respectable reputation want to become publicly associated with a subject so many people consider offensive? My own reasons are both professional and personal. I grew up in Daphne's world and married into Samantha's. In both environments, because of external circumstances and the limitations of my own personality, I was largely an observer. In my childhood I heard patronizing gossip from my parents about people who had "married well" and outright scorn for neighbors and members of the extended family who were rigorously grooming their children to do the same. ("Marrying well" is a euphemism for marrying up: to money, excellent career prospects and social position.) Without a challenging thought, I accepted the educational advantages and cultural frills I was given as necessary preparation for a useful and self-sufficient life. When I fell in love in my twenties, I would have been ashamed to consider whether or not the man had any money.

I married someone celebrated for distinguished artistic achievement. A few artists, like Picasso, become very rich. For others, artistic success becomes more of a money equivalent. With my husband, I entered a world of movers and shakers, wealth and achievement. I have dined at the president's table at the Kennedy and Johnson White Houses, visited informally at home with the two Pablos of twentieth century music and art—at Casals' summer quarters at Marlboro and at Picasso's villa at Notre Dame de Vie. I have been bored seated next to Huntingford Hartford at dinner and enchanted next to Adlai Stevenson at lunch. My present and past homes have been pictured in *Vogue*. I have been featured in *Women's Wear Daily*, along with Babe Paley, Audrey Hepburn and Gloria Guinness, as an example of the "ladylike look." I have ridden to hounds regularly, wearing the buttons of the hunt.

There were Rockefellers, Harrimans, Whitneys, Mellons and Vanderbilts at many of the receptions and celebrations we attended, as well as luminaries of the literary, art and entertainment worlds. But the names don't mean much. Most of the chairmen of the oil companies and the boards of regents, the major art collectors and donors of new galleries to museums, the founders of international organizations to help children, the owners of publishing and media empires, the expert shapers of economic and social policy, have names that are scarcely household words. A few of these people were my husband's friends. A few became my friends. Others remained highly visible acquaintances. I came to know the stories of many men and women who had married spouses a great deal wealthier than themselves. Some of these stories had happy outcomes. Others might serve as cautionary tales. Some offer examples of strategies that another person might duplicate.

Today, I understand that the scornful attitudes of moral superiority maintained by people like my parents are often defenses against disappointment and envy. My outlook is more attuned to the realities of the world in which I live. I understand that marriage is a mutual support system that works best when it functions on many levels. Social, career and financial considerations matter very much, along with the personal and sexual compatability emphasized in contemporary popular mythology. Marriage counselors have been reporting for years that more problems in marriages have to do with money than with sex.

## Layers of Truth

Professionally, my work as a therapist requires that I include in my explorations with patients the most hidden away, guilt-laden parts of their experiences and feelings. These often are concealed from an individual's own awareness, usually at some cost to the functioning of the person's mind and body. Depression, pessimistic outlook, irrational panic, lethargy, indecisiveness, repeated failures in work or in getting along with others, as well as a host of troublesome physical symptoms, are often the price of concealing "forbidden" thoughts and feelings from oneself. Optimal functioning in life—in work, play and relationships—comes from the capacity to be aware of all of one's wishes and motivations, combined with sufficient good judgment to decide when it is wise or worthwhile to act according to those wishes and when it is not.

At the turn of the century, when Freud discovered the healing possibilities that lay in having all of one's thoughts and feelings accepted, the major forbidden subject was sex. Today, in the detumescent phase of the sexual revolution, money—or one's personal relationship to money—often turns out to be a much more taboo subject. There are social situations in which people are more likely to reveal the intimate details of their sex lives than their income tax brackets. This may be so because it's easier to get away with lying about sex. But I believe it has to do more with the precariousness of immediate, individual survival. While sex is a pleasure and a necessity for the survival of the species in the future, some amount of money is necessary for most people's survival in the present.

One of the most self-sufficient men I've ever known lives along the coast of Maine. He can build a house or a boat from his own plans, catch fish, plant a vegetable garden or an orchard and put up preserves, make a crude fiddle and play it, cut and stack a whole winter's supply of firewood, and probably deliver a baby or set a simple fracture in an emergency. But he works as a caretaker for a rich man who owns an island off that coast—for money. There are taxes to pay on the woodland, fuel for the chain saw and tires for the pickup truck, medicine for the epileptic child, and the eyeglasses his wife needs to see what she's sewing. There are some things it is impossible, or too inefficient, to make for oneself.

The possession or control of large sums of money gives some people a great deal of power over other people. Certain individuals—often the grandfathers and grandmothers of today's public-spirited aristocrats—have done terrible things in order to acquire large sums of money. These associations help to charge the whole subject of money with magic, myth and ethical uncertainties. Money can represent superior strength, boundless pleasure, benevolence, love, sexual prowess, beauty, talent, health, wisdom and immortality. And money can represent every kind of hideous depravity.

Marrying money or its equivalents in power and position is a subject that becomes disreputable only when it is discussed publicly as a personal goal. Privately, in upper-class and many middle-class families, it is understood that marrying money or one of its equivalents is the most sensible course. The family social life accordingly is set up in a way that naturally steers the children in this direction. The gossip of the rich is laced with speculation about the sizes of other people's fortunes—how they were acquired, and how they are being spent. Yet talking about oneself directly in relation to money makes most of the people at polite dinner tables at least as squeamish as if a man were to start talking about the size of his penis or a woman about her preferences in coital positions.

A subject so loaded with fantasy and so linked to potency, morality and survival is one that fosters the development of multiple standards within an individual's thinking. A person can have one set of values and goals for public consumption, another set for private speculation, and a third, murkier set shaped by the kinks in his character and the gaps in his self-esteem. One aim of this book is to help its readers to allow themselves to know the full range of their feelings about money, as well as about marriage, so that money can be included openly in the list of attributes to be assessed in considering a potential mate. I am not advocating that a spouse's money or worldly position become the major priority. Marriages based only on money or upward mobility, with no other personal attraction or shared goals, can be quick routes to addiction, physical and mental illness, suicide, murder, or, at the very least, messy and bitter divorce. Money alone is not enough for a satisfactory life. But in combination with other things, it certainly can help.

Of course, money's place on the list of priorities will differ from one individual to another and for the same individual at different times. And each individual's capacity to attract money will vary. The purpose of this book is not to tell you that you *should* marry money or privileged position, but to open the subject to healthy, respectable exploration and provide some guidelines for further pursuit.

## Money and Morality

In our society, upward mobility is a tradition. It always has been considered praiseworthy to "pick a winner," "marry a comer," "get ahead." And this is not merely an American phenomenon. Historically, marriage usually has had to do with more sober and calculated issues than romance.

Few members of royal families have had the luxury of marrying anyone they pleased for love alone. The one who did most famously in this century, Edward VIII of England, gave up his throne for the privilege. (There always has been some speculation that he married for the privilege of giving up his throne.) Henry VIII, Napoleon, the Shah of Iran, and the heads of many lesser known dynasties, including industrial and financial empires, have divorced or otherwise disposed of wives who could not give them the heirs they required to preserve their power and possessions.

Many marriages in this country have been based on merging two plantations or ranches or shipping fleets or banking houses. In many of our most affluent suburbs, there is at least one dutiful daughter whose husband was selected by her father as a suitable choice for taking over the management of the family business. There are Orthodox Jews and Chinese Americans who are only one generation away from societies in which, whatever the economic level, it was accepted practice that parents knew best about choosing appropriate spouses for their sons and daughters.

In the nineteenth century, Henry James wrote realistically about American adventuresses and impoverished European noblemen who saw that their only chance to survive decently was to find a fortune to marry. Jane Austen's work, in which the poor, virtuous heroine and the rich, noble hero were united in true love after a series of misunderstandings, was the fiction of wish fulfillment. Her novels were written in an era in which women of all classes were without power or property and had to marry whatever man could provide the best living for them.

Today's popular public standard of marrying primarily for romantic love represents the ideal of a mobile, unhierarchical society in which everything is theoretically possible for everyone. In the middle classes, huge amounts of property and major inheritances are not at stake. Yet, even in this society, almost everybody's parents are supposed to have said, "It's as easy to fall in love with a rich girl—or a rich boy—as a poor one." (Many of the students attended my *How to Marry Money* classes had been sent by their parents.)

But the nature of competition and envy are such that, as soon as a spouse's or a potential spouse's money is mentioned, everyone else suspects that there is no love involved at all, simply a commercial transaction: body and soul for cold, hard cash.

The message is tricky but clear. It's all right to want to marry someone whose attributes include more money than you have, but be careful when and where you talk about it. You can mention wealth as one of the attractions of someone you are considering as a potential mate, but if you succeed in marrying the person, never mention the money again. Everybody wants to be loved, but nobody wants to be loved for his money. Or her money. And if you mention money, nobody will believe you love the person for any another reason.

So the Daphnes, female and male, who succeed in a deliberate drive to improve their financial and social positions through marriage, go underground. They will not share or compare their strategies with those whose training has not equipped them for such campaigns. However, in order to save her daughter from an impetuous "mistake," Daphne might admit, in a heated dialogue behind closed doors, that she had not fallen in love with Daddy at first sight but only came to appreciate his wonderful qualities after knowing him for a while. His loyalty, competence and dependability as a good provider would be listed as important virtues.

In the upper classes, speaking privately with intimates who share their understanding of society, people are more likely to acknowledge the importance of the money—or the privileges and buffers the money provides—in keeping a particular marriage together. There often is a high degree of contentment in such marriages. In this class, it is taken for granted that it is the elaborate structure, rather than two sets of finely tuned feelings for each other, that keeps most long-term marriages enduring. But to spend time discussing these private arrangements publicly is considered unnecessary and in poor taste, akin to a display of one's underwear.

## Training to Marry Up

Actually, Daphne and a number of other persons whose stories will turn up later are exceptions among those who think about marrying into a much richer class than the one in which they grew up. Most of the people who think it might be a good idea to marry up don't really want to do it. They have a vague idea. Someone else's life looks pleasant and effortless. Privileges and possessions are appealing, if only things would turn out that way. They really don't want to know about the training and discipline behind the scenes. For them marrying up is simply a daydream, wistful at times, resentful at others, and sometimes rejected with the distinct flavor of sour grapes.

It is easy to envy a woman I will call Pace Dollarson for her designer clothes and to poke fun at her "affected" speech when the evening news shows her breaking ground for the new museum wing to be named for her late husband, Mortimer, of the nine-digit fortune. It is harder to imagine oneself keeping appointments for fittings for that dress, negotiating with several cultural institutions for the best terms of endowment, consulting financial advisers on the sources from which the major contributions to the chosen museum will be funded.

It is even harder to imagine Pace's determined, velvet-gloved climb out of genteel obscurity. Her gracious charm is well known for being impervious to all reversals. What is not generally known are the countless private sorrows and humiliations that honed that wall of charm. Her stockpile of personal information, essential to operating smoothly among an intricately related throng of well-placed connections, has been amassed through diligent curiosity rendered automatic through years of practice and reinforced by several full Rolodex files. Pace was not young or inexperienced when she met and enchanted the elusive Mortimer Dollarson.

Most well-to-do families make some effort to instill in their children essential knowledge of the social ropes. When the Sunday lunch table habitually features Supreme Court justices, Nobel Prize winners, Cabinet members, university presidents, captains of industry and internationally acclaimed artists, the children get the message that the friendly garage mechanic or the pretty librarian just won't do. A woman who was sent to American and Swiss boarding schools from the age of seven reports that what she was trained to do best there was to pick out the most important man in any room and make herself indispensable to him. (She was also trained to return promptly the emerald earrings and any other baubles sent to her by a married suitor. The goal was not to become a successful courtesan.)

Old money families and those of more recent affluence join the best clubs they can get into. They send their children to the "right" camps and the "good" schools. Personal and business geneologies are enumerated at the dinner table or the breakfast table, and the children grow up aware of who owns what and who is related to whom. Traditions, old values, and the maintenance of standards are stressed. These references are not simply to pleasing table manners, intellectual excellence, cultural refinement or religious rectitude. Such qualities may matter, but they flourish most easily in environments in which money has initially provided the space and leisure for them to do so.

Marriage always has had as much to do with defining property and determining its orderly succession as with romance. Of course, it is usually all right if, within the approved circle, the son or daughter chooses the mate he or she personally finds most romantically appealing. But sometimes the stakes are too high or the opportunities too limited to allow even that much leeway.

## Rosalind the Doll

At sixteen, Rosalind—always so dainty and, after her nose job, so ethereally pretty—came crying to her one friend from the old neighborhood that her life was miserable, that she was constantly watched and was not allowed even to talk on the phone with a young man her parents didn't know and approve of. Her father was an ambitious dentist from Brooklyn with a talent for engaging in profitable forms of practice and investing in growth stocks. He had moved his family to a highly competitive and definitely *nouveau riche* suburb as his children approached marriageable ages. The dentist and his wife entertained with the expected show of luxury and gave expensive presents whenever appropriate. But the members of the community, mostly the children and grandchildren of Eastern European Jewish immigrants and assiduous climbers themselves, were as cautious in their approval of partners for their children as Rosalind's parents were. Rosalind had many more party dresses in her closet than she needed.

At nineteen, she married Simon. He was a surgeon, the son of a very successful wholesale furrier, and twelve years older than Rosalind. His parents, who had originally hoped for a more elevated match, were beginning to worry that he would never provide them with grandchildren. His interest in Rosalind came as a relief, so welcome that his parents supplied much more than the down payment on the great big doll's house in the suburb of Rosalind's father's choice. By that time, a home of her own, away from daily parental pressure and constraint, was very appealing to Rosalind.

Rosalind's life turned out to be everything her mother and father had wished. She entered wholeheartedly into her community's spirit of competitive conspicuous consumption, maintained her dainty figure, picked lint off the wall-to-wall carpeting of her frequently redecorated home, and raised her children to do at least as well as she had done herself. If her childhood friend were to turn up and remind her of her complaint at sixteen, she would probably give a sharp little snort at her adolescent naïveté and kiss the marble bathroom floor of her West Palm Beach vacation condominium in gratitude for her parents' good sense.

## For Men and Women: An Equal Opportunity Pursuit

The examples of Rosalind and Daphne may not appeal today to women who are no longer willing or able to count on succeeding entirely through their husbands. The approach is not limited to women, of course. Men with anything attractive about their persons or intellects always have been able to do well at marrying up, provided they don't aim unreasonably high. Traditionally men have been raised to get out in the world, pursue their goals actively, take the initiative in a variety of situations. This has operated in their favor in the marriage market as well as elsewhere.

Friends of Rosalind's parents had a son, Elliott, who was as lazy as he was devastatingly handsome. However, with repeated prompting from *his* ambitious father, Elliot managed to exert himself enough to woo and win the dumpy little daughter of a man known locally as the "mattress king." Elliott, with no particular vocational interests of his own, was presented to the mattress king as a budding businessman. A man was expected to do something other than be a mate and a parent. So, for Elliott, marriage meant instant partnership in a very successful bedding business, a comfortable enough spot for an indolent man, despite the needling vigilance of his father-in-law.

Other men and women combine independent achievement with wealthy marriages. Samantha got a graduate degree in social work and keeps on working to maintain a separate identity, as well as to have a hedge against the unpredictable future. Ambitious and intellectually gifted men frequently have been known to marry wealthy women whose money and connections smoothed the men's entries into outstanding careers or provided appropriate backgrounds to complement the men's achievements. Standard advice to young architects and would-be politicians is to marry rich women. Sometimes when there are no other heirs, a rich father picks out a less affluent young man in the approved social circle, a man the father feels he can trust with both his daughter and his business, and offers him a package deal.

Successful women in business and the arts frequently have married rich and powerful men. They have gained both the affectionate companionship of someone to whom their drive presents no threat and opportunities to advance in their own careers or social positions. It would be splitting hairs to try to isolate all the motives that blend in such matches. Obviously, those qualities of personal magnetism, energy and intelligence that lead to wealth and power often include genuine sex appeal.

A well-to-do Italian industrialist, Giovanni Battista Meneghini, provided an atmosphere in which his superbly gifted but impoverished young wife, Maria Callas, could concentrate on building her opera career. A divorcee named Leona Roberts was already an outstanding success in the real estate business when she married Harry Helmsley, New York's top real estate man, but life with the man described by the press as owning a quarter of New York's skyline could not help but enlarge her horizons in the business.

In or out of the spotlight, there are many capable and achieving men and women who simply never would have been attracted to a spouse whose desirable personal characteristics were not enhanced by occupying a position of leadership or power. A person with drive and ambition is not likely to be satisfied to share the life of someone who expects him or her to keep a low profile.

## Too High a Price?

For those who are not already firmly committed, it may sound, on the basis of some of the preceding examples, as if the price of marrying up is too high. No wonder that most people don't follow through. But consider: Was Elliott's father-in-law worse than the bosses he might have had to deal with if he had tried to make his own way up the business ladder? Was Rosalind, never noted for brains or talent, more bored picking lint off the carpets of her expensive homes than she would have been if she had eloped with the handsome football player she had had a crush on in high school? (The best job the football player has ever had is assistant manager of a men's discount clothing store, and he spends more evenings out with his bowling league than out with his wife or at home in their rent-stabilized apartment.)

Was being a cultural leader in her community less satisfying to Daphne than scrambling for low-paid posts on college or high school music faculties? For every cautionary tale about the terrible personal cost of marriage to a rich person, there are a dozen horror stories about marriage to anyone at all. Sophie Tucker said, "I've been rich, and I've been poor, and rich is better." Someone else amended it: "I've been unhappy rich, and I've been unhappy poor, and rich is better."

Naturally, marriage is not the only route to acquiring the kind of money, power or position that defines the difference between struggle and endeavor, comfort and luxury, settling and choosing, service and command. Making a success on one's own can give a tremendous boost to morale and life style in a number of important ways. But having money oneself, or achieving something notable, does not necessarily bar the additional enhancement of marrying someone who also has money and status, and perhaps more of them. In fact, having money or one of its equivalents usually makes marrying up easier and more appropriate.

## Theme and Variations

Rosalind, Elliott, Daphne, Samantha and Pace are examples of different types of affluence with different behavioral and material standards. They offer guidelines for the diverse attitudes found among the great variety of people who have money and position.

Rosalind, Elliott and Daphne were coached toward their marital careers from childhood. Samantha's was a spontaneous extension of natural endowment and events that shaped her early life. Pace represents a rarefied phenomenon predictable in certain environments. Usually, at least one parent of a woman like Pace can claim a background of aristocratic comfort and refinement. But something has gone wrong. Perhaps the other parent's manners or occupation are below standard. Or perhaps there is simply no money any more. Throughout her childhood, through the fallen parent's litany of memories and references, Pace is coached to get out, to move back up where she "belongs," and where, thanks to the parent's background, she knows the language and the ways.

Daphne and Philip. Samantha and Greg. Rosalind and Simon. Pace and Mortimer. Those are not their real names, of course. Neither are Hilda and Dan, Ben and Meg, Myron and Edith, or most of the other names that will turn up in these pages. Most of them aren't even real people but composites of many individuals who represent characteristics I want to illustrate.

This is not a "who's who" but an exploration of how,

when and why people marry up. The stories offer some examples of the circumstances, and the kinds of people, that make such marriages successful, and some of those that don't. They also offer a range for measuring yourself, seeing whether you are the kind of person who marries up, whether you might become that kind of person, and whether or not you really would want to be.

# 2

## Money and Its Equivalents

### Assets

When we say someone has money, we are using a symbolic term for an accumulation of possessions of value. Those possessions could be deposits in banks, ownerships or shares of businesses, real estate, livestock, minerals, objects or commodities of every description from fine art and vintage wine to sable skins, lumber, silicone chips and heavy machinery. We could be referring to relatively predictable income from high salaries or fees or to expected future income from loans, bonds, speculative investments, insurance policies, pensions and trust funds.

However, much of what attracts us as wealth does not really have to do with the current ownership of material goods or money. We see certain behavior, achievements, connections, and we think "money." Very often, we are observing other assets—what I call "money equivalents"—in action. These can come from a family background that gives automatic standing in a community or easy access to important and influential individuals. Extra endowments of brains, beauty, talent, energy, wit, resilience, or any characteristic that enables one person to do more than another in the same situation, to attract more favorable attention or to acquire greater privileges can be a money equivalent. Any form of power is a money equivalent.

Money equivalents can be the perquisites of a particular job that allow someone to use expensive facilities which are paid for by the company. These perks may include cars, chauffeurs, airplanes, apartments, generous expense accounts, memberships in country clubs and lunch clubs, and travel allowances for spouses on business trips. Other job perquisites function as money equivalents by freeing up income through having the company supply or pay for necessities, such as sophisticated insurance policies, extensive health benefits, personal legal services, financial counseling and school tuitions, that someone else would have to buy for himself or herself.

In companies that compete for high level employees, the range of perks can cover all areas of life. The higher up the corporate scale and the more valued the employee is, the more individually tailored and imaginative the perks become. However, the situation can get out of hand, even for the boss. Some stockholders of the Ford Motor Company once sued its chairman, Henry Ford II, for fifty million dollars in damages, claiming that he misused corporate funds for political dinners and personal luxuries. There are money equivalents connected with work but not usually listed as perks. These can include minor items such as personal use of phones and office supplies. They certainly include the major amounts of time that can be freed when one or more secretaries take over personal chores such as balancing a checkbook or selecting presents for family members or when specialized assistants such as draftsmen, copy editors and statisticians handle portions of complex assignments.

## Cash and Class

Money can also be described socially by categories having to do with length of possession, modes of behavior, what shows and what never is mentioned. Old Money and New Money are familiar terms. Old Money usually has been in the family for more than two generations. New Money could have been acquired within the last year or the last generation. Manner and milieu keep it "New."

Old Money can be divided further into the Useful Rich and the Useless Rich. The Useful Rich have a sense of social responsibility, particularly toward those less fortunate than themselves. In these families, direct participation in useful work is encouraged. The children often become doctors, social workers, lawyers and teachers. They focus on some aspect of social inequity or service to the disadvantaged. These families establish philanthropic foundations and stay involved in their activities. "Contribution" means more substantial effort than buying tickets to charity balls. The Useless Rich live only for their own pleasure. Since a perpetual state of pleasure is humanly impossible, the results of their doomed strivings to sustain nirvana/euphoria often turn up in the scandal sheets and the courts.

There is a subcategory of Old Money often referred to as No Money. The No Money Rich are from good old families. They might be penniless, but No Money in their circles more often means that they have nothing left but the nine-room cottage on a ten-acre corner of the old estate, or they are down to the last, uninvadable trust fund, and an income only twice as large as that of an experienced executive secretary. Even if they really are without funds, their social style often appeals to the upwardly mobile. And if a No Money person is bright and ambitious, the old family connections still offer access to promising job opportunities.

New Money can be divided into Snob Money, Slob Money and the Statustocracy. The goal of Snob Money is to become assimilated into the aristocracy (or whatever the Snob Money person perceives as aristocracy) as quickly as possible. Complete success often takes two generations, but, in the meantime, much expense and research, with rigorous attention to detail, are poured into duplicating the look, the manner, the settings and attitudes of Old Money.

Slob Money belongs to people who have made a lot of money and like to enjoy it but don't aspire to any particular social group. If they move to a new house or a spread of land, they do so because the place appeals to them for subjective reasons. They don't change their appearance or their ways to conform to the new surroundings. They may prefer to retain their old habits and friends in the same neighborhood, simply adding more comforts and services and, sometimes, making more contributions to the community. When a cottage industry has burgeoned into a national chain that's hot on the stock market, the down-home multimillionaire who started it may become a major contributor and lay leader of the church he always has attended, or he may devote more time and a new engine to the local volunteer fire department. The rock star may buy two floors of a stylish coop apartment building, but he still wears torn T-shirts and doesn't give sit-down dinner parties. The spending styles of Slob Money can be loud and vulgar, or they can be quiet and thoughtful, or just plain down-home, or anything in between. Slob Money people often are easier to meet and get along with than Old Money or Snob Money people, because their locations remain accessible and their customs remain familiar to someone who never has had the experience of living at the top socially.

The Statustocracy is actually a subgroup of Snob Money. Membership is based on the ability to transmit an impression of success and excellence according to the standards of the moment in the target group. Money, talent, power, style and social connections can be used interchangeably as points of advantage. The Statustocrats are not interested in the slow route to aristocracy. They are more concerned with the instant importance conferred by celebrity, by publicly recognized achievement, and by knowing where to be when and with what "look." Their spending patterns are competitive and highly sensitive to shifts in fashion, although part of the game is to pretend that one is above fashion.

## How Much and What For?

While there are substitutes for money, and there are desirable things that money can't buy, there is still a significant relationship between the possession of money and the ability to do or to have a great many things that matter. Anyone interested in acquiring money, through marriage or other means, should know what he wants money for. That is, what do you want to *do* with the money? And just how much money is required for the things you have in mind? If you want to turn a fantasy into reality, you start by getting to know the fantasy thoroughly.

People often say they want money so that they can do anything they want to do. That's fine, but what is anything? And what does it cost? For many individuals a major appeal of the money fantasy is being able to work only when they want to work. Others think about traveling. Others want to lie in the sun or follow their favorite sport or season around the globe.

Some people crave excitement, glamorous friends and heaps of luxurious things: cars, boats, airplanes, clothes, the latest electronic gadgets, jewels. Some want to pursue an art or learn a new skill. A few want money to promote a cause, follow an ideal, make a political or social welfare organization work. Some want to be able to provide decently for children and send them to good schools. Some want to be respected

in a certain community. Some think about a serene old age
for themselves or for relatives, and they count in the cost of
excellent medical and nursing care.

Many people would be glad to settle for living pretty
much the way they do now but without constant scrimping
and saving or having to treat every substantial purchase as
a major balancing act. All they ask is to be able to get their
teeth fixed and take a vacation away in the same year. Or
buy both the burgundy sweater and the gray one without
always having to choose.

In my *How to Marry Money* classes, a rising young employee of a conglomerate whose holdings included oil tankers
said that, to her, money meant billions. To many of the guests
lining up for buffet supper at a large Park Avenue duplex
after an art exhibition opening, it appeared that the income
from a six-million-dollar trust fund would do nicely. In a
gathering of young, middle-management men and women,
a salary of over a hundred thousand dollars a year meant
enviable success. An older woman who for many years had
seemed comfortably fixed in her handsome town and country
houses surprised me by saying that ten thousand a year more
than she now had would do; she was not interested in major
changes in her life, but that sum would pay for some minor
practical improvements. A struggling young actress reported
that wealth to her would mean being able to afford to buy
big, hardcover books whenever she wanted them. Many middle-class people simply would like to be able to count on
something more in old age than a shaky Social Security check.

Clearly, the fantasy of money is not always one of a great
fortune. (And a great fortune never could become a reality
for the majority of people.) Any kind of increase in spending
power counts as moving up financially. Many of the people
I have heard from could translate only part of their dream
into dollars. They are seeking an intangible difference in the
way life feels. That difference could have to do with roots,

status or recognition, with a certain ease in the daily mechanics of life or a particular style in dealing with other people. But whether it is for modest comfort or multimillions, a swath of luxury or a dignified old age, the first task for anyone hoping to turn the money fantasy into reality is to be specific.

## Pricing the Dream

When I asked the *How to Marry Money* students to estimate the cost of a very comfortable life, a young woman, previously identified as a rich man's wife who did not handle the bills herself, came up with fifty thousand a year. Other students, not rich but in charge of their own finances, groaned in protest. A general consensus from each class was that, in major cosmopolitan centers, one could not consider oneself well-to-do on less than a hundred thousand a year, preferably after taxes, and that in order to qualify as wealthy, an annual income from a wisely invested three to six million dollars' capital would be a realistic figure—particularly if there were children. (That is, from a hundred and fifty to three hundred thousand a year and up, depending on how conservative and how successful the investments are.) However, many of the participants in that consensus suspected that they would never achieve such incomes, and few had arrived at these figures by adding up the costs of specific things that mattered most to them.

When I asked the students to do a fantasy exercise that included picturing a wealthy residence, most of them came up with a particularly spacious place staffed with at least one servant. But it was harder to get them to think about what it would actually cost to buy that establishment and run it. No matter what a person wants and what he thinks of his chances, if he or she has any serious ambition at all, it won't do to say a "nice house" or a "comfortable life style." What size house? Where is it located? How many people can live there, and what can they do there? Are there outbuildings and other facilities: stables, greenhouses, tennis courts, swimming pools, cottages for guests or employees?

Whether it's a complete estate, a simple country cottage, or a stylish nest in town, you must consider maintenance costs, taxes, insurance, furnishings and decorations, the cost of food and drink, housekeeping supplies and services. There are other costs that go with living in a particular community, particularly if one is interested in belonging there rather than simply coexisting. In each kind of place there are some services, possessions, memberships that can be purchased in order to facilitate the comfortable life style appropriate to the place. Sometimes certain conveniences and privileges are not available to newcomers or not to those without the right credentials. In some communities, private clubs and residential enclaves still remain restricted to certain ethnic groups or limited to openings by inheritance or by recommendation of old members. In many places, tradesmen and mechanics give preferential treatment to "old families" and ignore newcomers. A well-maintained residence, church attendance, large contributions to community causes, and a reserved seat in the commuter express car may not penetrate the polite aloofness maintained toward unknown new arrivals who do not look or sound "right."

Homework about basic costs can be done fairly easily through reading, phone calls and some legwork. It is feasible to consult real estate brokers, travel agents, caterers, insurance brokers, automobile and boat dealers, domestic employment agencies, landscape gardeners—anyone whose services or products cover some aspect of the life one has in mind. Some of this information is available in magazine articles and newspaper ads. It is not impracticable to check on the costs as well as the accessibility of club memberships and school tuitions, or to find out how much it takes to become a significant supporter of local cultural institutions. It is instructive to read restaurant menus and tipping guides, and visit art galleries, antique shops and quality stores, if their goods are part of the fantasy. It is not difficult to price the clothing, the accessories, the home furnishings, vehicles, sports paraphernalia and any other equipment that belongs in a particular dream. It is possible to find out what sums of money—and other credentials—one is dreaming about.

## Wealth on a Sliding Scale

Like beauty, money is often in the eye of the beholder. What a person imagines is limited by what he or she has experienced and observed. Observation can come from books, movies, magazines, grandmother's memories, window shopping or neighborhood gossip, but it has to come from somewhere. To the bookkeeper for a rural hardware store, the telephone in the marble bathroom of a metropolitan hotel may be the height of luxury. To a high fashion dress buyer, that same hotel's failure to provide terry cloth bathrobes and fresh flowers in the room is a distinct comedown. The dress buyer's standard is based on past observation. The bookkeeper's standard is in the process of being expanded by the present experience.

Sometimes, it can be better not to have observed too many possibilities. In Alexander Solzhenitsyn's novel, *The Cancer Ward*, the hero's whole view of his life is shattered by one such experience. The middle-aged political exile, wandering the streets of a provincial Eurasian town after leaving the hospital where his life has been saved, smells shashlik being roasted over an open fire. When he tastes the roast meat for the first time, he realizes how poor he is. Until then, he had considered himself rich because he had had a university education. Until then, he had believed that a piece of freshly baked black bread was the finest eating experience to which a man could aspire.

Even within the same culture, a dozen different individuals will have a dozen different ideas of what "rich" means. Daphne, married to Philip, the successful professional man, made a splash in her middle-American town with a living room that doubled as a small concert hall. To Philip's father, a sturdy, seven-room house on an acre of land in a quiet residential neighborhood suggested a family of substance. To Mortimer Dollarson, scion of a great fortune, that house barely would have done for the gardener's cottage. To Cerelia, a welfare mother of three living on the deteriorating fringes of the South Bronx—or to Laurie June, her Appalachian counterpart—two bedrooms, a kitchen separate from the living room, and a tiled bathroom would be almost more luxury than she would dare to imagine.

To Philip and Daphne's daughter, "good" clothes mean things from the better sportswear department of a suburban branch of a well-known specialty store. To Pace Dollarson's niece, that kind of shopping is slumming. For Rosalind and Simon, evidence of wealth lies in entertaining with good vermeil flatware and lavish presentations of food. Their son, about to graduate from an Ivy League college, is beginning to suspect that being rich has something to do with buying contemporary paintings, knowing people who make government policy, and being comfortable with shorthand foreign travel references at the dinner table.

The same amounts of money can be spent in very different ways. People who appear to be of the same class and living in the same way often will turn out to be operating on very different incomes. These variations have to do with personal tastes and priorities, natural endowment, old habits and current ambitions. Rosalind and Samantha both have the kinds of looks and ways of dressing that turn heads. Rosalind's yearly salon bills for the care of hair, skin, nails and body would support a family of four at better than the poverty level. Samantha gets a wash and wear haircut every six weeks, and her entire stock of cosmetics would fit in a regulation post office box. But Samantha buys one-of-a-kind costumes from boutiques when they strike her fancy, while Rosalind watches for sales in the better stores and patronizes a "little woman" who sells designer lingerie out of her apartment at below wholesale prices. (Rosalind's son, Jeffrey, wants money for books, concert tickets, some rare lithographs, a movie camera and time to develop an idea he has for a documentary. He has discovered the cultural branch of the Statustocracy.)

Rosalind's sister-under-the-skin, Barbara, owns a glass-walled architectural statement in a fashionable country village and a sleek, lacquered looking apartment in town in which comfort and function are sacrificed consistently to a stylish look. She carries her big cooking pots back and forth. They don't show. Barbara's neighbor, Jessica, has a modestly furnished apartment and a small cottage in the country, but she has thousands of dollars' worth of the most efficient cooking utensils money can buy in both places. Her priority is convenience.

Some differences in the spending power of similar assets have to do with the amount of freebies or perks or money equivalents available to an individual because of historic connections, desirable personal attributes, or the opportunities for special arrangements. When Samantha and Greg renovated the coach house, Greg arranged for his company to pick up part of the costs, on the basis that the house would be used for substantial business entertaining. Greg and Samantha usually can get the company plane to take them to and from their ski weekends. Abroad, they stay in luxury hotel suites maintained by the firms with which Greg does business.

Greg, Philip, and Rosalind's husband, Simon, might all admit, if you insisted on asking, that they were "comfortable." None would think of himself or herself as rich. All could point to someone much richer. Mortimer Dollarson probably would have done the same, and his estate was valued at over a hundred million dollars. The image of "money" is hard to pin down. One man's fortune is another's small change. And one man's small change is another's ransom.

## Dollars and Sense

Sometimes when people say they want money, they really are thinking about something else. They may mean a position of respect, fame or adulation, political power, or the ability to influence events and get their way with other people. They may believe that having what money can buy will make them feel loved. They may believe it will make them safe and secure for the rest of their lives.

Money can play a part in all these designs, but it is never the whole picture. Being a member of a respected family in the community may have more to do with a past fortune than a present one. If your great-grandfather once owned most of the land on which the town was built; your grandfather was founder and president of the bank; and your father became a state supreme court judge, you are "somebody" in that town, even if you lose your teaching job, don't bathe very often, and take three months to pay your grocery bills. It's possible to become "somebody" in a community by endowing a library or donating an entire hospital wing, but the New Money donor may not feel as nobly entrenched as he had hoped. Some determined types load the dice by first making the money to endow the library and then marrying that un-employed son or daughter of the family who already receives the deference they seek. (Of course, if you only want a feeling of membership without exalted status there are less expensive ways to participate and become accepted in a geographic or philosophical community.)

Many people focus on a single obstacle to happiness and begin to believe that if only this one problem were solved, everything about their lives would be wonderful. They become so obsessed with one particular flaw that they lose sight of all the dissatisfactions and irritations from other sources. If only I could fix the bump on my nose, they say... or lose thirty pounds... find a great apartment... have an orgasm... postpone my ejaculation... find someone who understands me... meet some interesting people... find a job I could be proud of... get my hands on a million dollars, then I'd feel marvelous. If they fix the nose or get their hands on the million dollars, then they begin to notice what else is missing.

Money can be a very useful tool. It can buy time through a battery of supportive services. It can buy space and other physical comforts. It can supply screens and buffers from a rude and dangerous world. It can buy soothing luxuries, amusing distractions, excellent educational opportunities, the best medical care. It can free an individual to choose activities that really interest him rather than his having to grab the highest paying job he can get simply to survive. Money can purchase access to sophisticated information and the finest equipment for work or play. It can buy expert advice on any subject and skilled assistance in improving a person's appearance, sound, style and state of mind. Money spent on pleasing and supporting others can sometimes even buy a semblance of love and loyalty. Money can do a lot, but it is not a cure-all.

No amount of money can guarantee a secure future. Fortunes evaporate. Tornadoes strike. Bullets explode. Cars go out of control. Love turns to hate. Cancer metastasizes. Children drown. People can be informed and watchful and prudent. They can influence their environment but they never can entirely control it. When a person's sense of security is based entirely on money, it is false. Security comes from developing one's abilities and accepting one's limitations, planning realistically but being willing to cope with the unexpected.

There is a human quality known as self-love. It comes

from respect and liking for the person one really is. It has nothing to do with the insistent, self-centered puffery of pathological narcissism. (The narcissist says he's wonderful, but he feels terrible. The person who really loves himself may not mention it, but he feels pretty good.) This quality, self-love, comes about as close as people can get in this world to permanent, portable security. However, inner security does not cancel out the desirability of the comforts, pleasures and conveniences that money can buy. It just helps to keep them in reasonable perspective. It also can function as a money equivalent because it frees the energy that others spend on worrying about themselves, and it makes its possessor very appealing to many people, including the rich and successful.

# 3

# Why Would "Money" Marry You?

### The Rich Singles' Choice

E verybody knows that rich people marry other rich people. Operating on the theory that one never can have too much of a good thing, the very rich often like to marry the very much richer. Or they look for symbols of splendor beyond money. Noble and royal titles used to qualify, but even though three American women have married reigning monarchs since World War II, title hunting is not very much in style any more. Perhaps Wallis Warfield Simpson retired the game. Only the bored old Useless Money rich bother with titles now. To be serious marriage material these days, foreigners have to be rich themselves. New Money Americans are interested in power, celebrity, or being absorbed into the American aristocracy. So the old rich marry each other, and the new rich marry the old rich when they can.

People who are reasonably contented with the lives they lead marry people who are not likely to disrupt those lives excessively. Less contented people are more inclined to seek others who appear to offer something that will enhance their lives dramatically. For the less than rich, money has obvious potential as a life enhancer. But there are other things that appeal occasionally to people of all degrees of wealth. What they are depends partly on the individual's characteristics, including self-image and fantasies, and partly on the standards of the particular segment of society that matters to that individual. Specific talents or skills, certain kinds of appearance or style, unusual personal qualities, or a set of strategic connections or high status associations all can have value in the marrying up market. Timing plays a part, too.

## The Trouble with Outsiders

The rich try to be on guard against those whose interest in them has to do mostly with their fortunes. One does not have to be really rich to be subject to this hazard. A rising account executive with a three-room apartment and a steady salary can be very appealing to a frequently unemployed copywriter who would rather stay home and dream up screenplays impossible to produce. To Cerelia, the welfare mother, the owner of a fast food stand with two sets of books at a rundown public beach represents lavish wealth. Many mismatches among the poor endure, miserably, because one partner's little bit of wages represents the only shield between the other and destitution. But when there is a substantial amount of money that no one has to work for—and the more money there is, the more this is so—its possessors are concerned about maintaining control of that money and seeing that it is preserved within the family from generation to generation. If you can pass that control on to your descendants, or exert it yourself through wills and trusts for several generations, you are extending your power beyond your own life span. It is a potent step toward immortality.

Fortune hunters can strike from within rich families' own circles as well as from without, but the outsiders are more obvious. Insiders are more likely to know the rules and settle for a secure living arrangement and the prospect of wealthy children than try to indulge dreams of controlling a great fortune themselves. While the code talk among the rich of maintaining high family standards and good values has to do with money, it also has to do with everyone's fear of strangers and the unknown. If money cannot buy some safety, some promise of adherence to comfortable guidelines in a precarious world, what good is it? So the rich marry the rich not only to preserve their fortunes but also to assure a serene, predictable path for their lives. To be tolerated by the old rich, a newcomer has to take on some of the protective co-loration of their manners, values, and vocabulary.

Even the most democratically minded children of the rich find themselves separated from the non-rich by forces they do not set in motion themselves. They may go to public school for a while, or at private schools mingle with scholarship students. But while all the children can share what happens at school, the rich children's experiences away from school may be too different for the others to comprehend.

The rich children are accustomed to spacious homes, serv-ants, antiques, art, lavish or multiple vacation homes, clubs, sophisticated sports facilities, frequent and comfortable travel. They have parents, grandparents, aunts and uncles with busi-ness and social connections to interesting and important peo-ple. They have familiar, everyday access to quality goods and services. Good manners and taste are part of their everyday lives (though there are many flagrant exceptions). They get repeated acknowledgment from their environment that they belong to a select group of people who "matter" in the world. They look forward to assured futures of trust funds, family businesses and interesting opportunities. The rich children may be friendly to the other children, but they build up frames of reference not available to the others. By the time they are grown up and ready to rear children of their own, they simply are more comfortable with those who share their own context of options and associations.

For one thing, it's safer not to evoke envy and resentment. For another, it's more fun not to have to worry about hurting other people's feelings. At the college I attended, a democratic approach to living arrangements was imposed so vigorously that it was difficult to tell the rich students from the poor ones, even on more than superficial acquaintance. In the spring of my senior year, when the privilege of keeping a car on campus finally became available, many students bemoaned the fact that they couldn't afford a car. But one of my classmates finally said, "I'm sick of pretending to be poor! I'm rich. I can afford a car, a brand new one, and I'm glad of it!"

A little later on in my youth, I was a guest in the mansion of a dowager whose seventy-fifth birthday was being celebrated with a black-tie dinner. Women in that cosmopolitan city were accustomed to wearing long evening dresses to such parties. But the other woman houseguest and myself had brought the short cocktail dresses that were customary in our more provincial circles. Our wardrobes were known to the hostess because her maid had unpacked for us. When we came downstairs to leave for the party, there she was, bejeweled and dazzling, but in a short dress. Some members of her family commented in surprise on her choice. They were quickly silenced. Though they would not have dared to say so, their feelings must have resembled my classmate's outburst.

The dowager, in *her* youth an impoverished, intellectual beauty who had married a wealthy financier, had spent her life creating a grand hearth for the brilliant and talented, regardless of origins and economic position. She was accustomed to providing the guest rooms, the food, the transportation, and sometimes more substantial support, for those interesting and attractive people who were not in her husband's financial league. Partly the *noblesse oblige* style of another, richer era, her generosity was not motivated entirely by altruism. This habitual thoughtfulness toward a circle of brains and varied achievement had provided stimulating companionship and a particular kind of social distinction for her husband and herself. Descended from educated and moderately successful people, but not of the old guard WASP aristocracy, they had cleared their own path to parallel eminence.

But most rich people don't want to have to pay their friends' way. If you are witty, attractive and well-mannered, they might be delighted to have you join them at the expertly staffed restaurants and secluded resorts they frequent, but not if they always have to pick up the check. And your uneasy lack of familiarity with the way things are done on the rare occasions when you can afford to join them does not contribute to anyone's enjoyment. Knowing how to behave and what to expect offers a charming serenity. Why jar it? So most of the rich find it more agreeable to spend their time with those who share their vocabularies and their habits.

## When Rich Sons and Daughters Marry Out

Yet, not all the rich who have grown up rich are comfortable within their own economic circles. Sometimes ethnicity or the wrong religion has barred them from the really inner sanctums of clubs, residential compounds, or the old boy networks of top school and firms. Sometimes family scandals or severe financial losses have expelled them. Sometimes parental neglect or tyranny or the cruelty of servants who looked after them has warped the development of their personalities and left them bewildered and resentful. In a spouse, they want compensation for past wrongs. They may believe they are seeking warmth, comfort, protection, but in one way or another, they actually look for someone to impress and dominate.

A troublesome issue that emerges frequently is that of competition with a dominant, spectacularly achieving parent. The son of a Wall Street wizard may decide to become an epidemiologist, an experimental farmer, or a dabbler in literature and the arts rather than face having to measure himself against his powerful father in traditional business circles. To remove himself further from the competitive pressures of his own background, he may deliberately seek a wife who is an outsider. Perhaps she will be someone whose style and associations will help him blend into the undistinguished middle class of his chosen colleagues. Or she is outstanding but foreign or of a different race, or the possessor of an obvious, lower-class accent and manner.

Or she may be someone whose position his parents consider clearly subservient: the *au pair* girl, a nurse from a small farm family, the fashion model who was a high school dropout. The Rockefeller family comes so easily to mind. Winthrop, son of the original founder of the fortune, John D., married a miner's daughter and movie bit player, Bobo Palekiute Sears, who lived, when he met her, in a walk-up, cold water flat. A decade later, Winthrop's nephew Steven (son of the serious United States presidential contender, Nelson) married his mother's maid, Anne Marie Rasmussen, a grocer's daughter from Norway.

In psychoanalytic terms, bypassing adult competition with the father is an attempt to evade the classical oedipal issue: The son who tries to surpass his father (and take his place with mother) has to kill the father or be killed by him. In emotional development, unlike Greek myth, this does not mean actual incest and murder but a series of fierce internal conflicts to be experienced and resolved as a normal part of the growing-up process. The function of the oedipal conflict is to prepare the child to come to terms with his parents as a respectful but independent adult. The son who chooses a low-key career and a wife whom he perceives as an "inferior" really may have a love for farming and no aptitude for banking, but he also may be attempting to avoid the whole oedipal challenge. He accepts being less powerful permanently, and he remains psychically connected to his parents as a dependent child. He still is intensely in need of his father's approval and his mother's continuing protection.

Normal resolution of the oedipal situation would require the man to marry a woman "as good as" his mother. So, in choosing a wife who cannot compete with his mother as a social equal, he has challenged neither his mother's nor his father's supremacy in his life. The woman who marries a rich man in this emotional position should be prepared to deal with a substantial amount of disguised infantile needs. Among the forms of expression these may take are indecisiveness, easily hurt feelings, petty retaliation and rapid alternation between possessive and rejecting behavior.

Of course, many sons of aggressive, successful fathers accept the challenge and willingly model their vocational and personal careers on their fathers'. But sometimes the father's performance has been outstanding in a way that is not particularly admirable or is not appropriate to the circumstances of the present generation. The father may have been a flamboyant sportsman, womanizer, alcoholic or gambler. Inflation and too many heirs may have eaten away much of the fortune. So the young man decides on a realistic adaptation. He embarks on a respectable career and chooses a sensible woman from a more modest background. He relies on her judgment to guide them into a stable family life and reasonable spending habits.

When a rich man makes a *second* marriage to a much poorer outsider after a first marriage within the approved or useful circle, this step can represent confidence and self-knowledge, or it can signify a late rebellion. However, the latter need usually can be satisfied through liaisons other than marriage. The rich *young* man whose wife is a social inferior, selected for revenge on his parents or domination of his environment, often dumps her or gets dumped on the grounds of cruel treatment. Emotional problems expressed through the symptoms of alcoholism or other addiction, secondary impotence, promiscuity, and sadistic treatment are not reserved exclusively for the rich. But the presence of wealth allows for more extravagant expression and more expensive compensation.

The patterns for rich women who need to defy the expectations of their families are somewhat different. The available examples of success and prominence most often have been their fathers. A woman who has strongly identified with her father and modeled her career ambitions on his may have little tolerance for the demanding minutiae of daily life with a traditional husband. When there has been an outstanding mother with whom the daughter has had to compete, the mother more often has achieved her power base on looks and sex appeal or sturdy, altruistic caretaking than on vocational achievement outside the home. The daughters of some dominant women with very successful careers—either the traditional ones of homemaker and hostess or the historically less usual ones of professional, artistic or business success—have been known to respond like the sons of some overachieving fathers. Unwilling to compete directly, they develop along obviously different paths.

A famous, professional beauty's daughter may become a somber research scientist or a frowzy housewife. A renowned hostess with a penchant for extravagant attention-seeking and romantic self-indulgence may produce a daughter who is a self-effacing model of modest, organized logic and efficiency. An honored scientist may have daughters who drop out of school and flounder about on the most unproductive fringes of artistic circles. However, in my observation, unless the mother has been monstrously self-absorbed and rejecting, or ruthlessly destructive, any sort of model of achievement in the mother ultimately has been beneficial to the daughter and has contributed to her making something worthwhile out of her life, even if this happens late, after several false starts and mismatched marriages.

A "poor little rich girl" may find it is only her money, her father's connections, or even her mother's famous charm that attracted her husband. But the rich woman who has made such a mistake in her marriage through adolescent defiance or a reflection of her sad-sack self-image finds it easier than the poor one to correct her mistake and dump the man if he proves to be impossible when she is ready to assume her grown-up, self-respecting place in the world. At least, if she has not been disinherited, she has an income to fall back on.

## Matrimonial Addition

One of the problems in any marriage, even in our uprooted and mobile society, is that one does not usually have to deal only with the individual one marries. In addition to the spouse there are family, friends of all vintages and business associates. The higher the economic and social bracket and the bigger the leap the newcomer has made into it, the greater will be the distaste expressed by the rich spouse's circle and the more attempts made to discredit the newcomer. Disinheritance of the rich spouse is not unknown. Tolerating the barbs and aversion concealed barely, if at all, under a superficial politeness requires a very thick skin.

Sometimes a well-behaved outsider is made more welcome if he or she takes a defective offspring off the family's hands. An ideal example of such a situation was the basis of the movie, *Arthur*, in which the heir to an unimaginably vast fortune squandered his energy in a decadence that actually was quite innocent and impotent. He left all matters of coping with reality to his butler. As the butler entered the terminal stages of illness, Arthur met a sincere young working-class woman brimming with vitality and coping skills. Naturally, he had to fall in love and marry her, so that she could take over the butler's job of dealing with the world for him. The movie implies that she will teach him to cope. In real life, this kind of marital role is better suited to a stolid, patient person.

A truer to life example is the story of Myron and Edith. Edith, the third of four children in a wealthy and powerful family, was born with a scoliosis, a lateral curvature of the spine, too severe to be corrected significantly by surgery or physical therapy. Restricted in her movement, she was unintentionally neglected by her active, competitive family. Long before adolescence, she withdrew into an isolated emotional standstill that made her appear to be of less than average intelligence. While not exactly an embarrassment at the dinner table, Edith grew up physically awkward and intellectually dull. She did not enjoy a sparkling social life. The family urged her to find something to do. Through one of their connections, she got a "little" job at the natural history museum, helping to file bones and other small zoological specimens. At work, she met Myron, an assistant curator considered a failure by his middle-class family because he had opted for a Ph.D. in physical anthropology rather than medical school. Myron was more comfortable with dead animal specimens than with live, demanding human beings. Edith was tolerably quiet at work, and Myron was informed about her family. He began paying some guarded attention, took her out to dinner, got her home early.

Edith, flattered by the attention, decided she must be in love. Her limitations made her unthreatening and appealing to Myron. While not ruthlessly ambitious, he was no fool about survival. If his wife was not personally demanding, and her fortune could provide a house big enough for a quiet study for himself, servants to run it smoothly, and tuition for the children's education, he had no objection at all to being a married man of substance. The substance even could be parlayed into a modest professorship.

After several years of excitement at filling the wife and mother roles she had considered unattainable, Edith began to notice that Myron was not a particularly interesting or interested companion. She became unhappy, took the children away a lot to tour the wonders of several continents. But no one else was interested in Edith, either, except for some obviously sleazy types. And Myron, conversationally dull and blind to social refinement as he was, had his virtues. He was always there, didn't pay attention to other women, didn't drink or gamble, and had some affection for the children. So the marriage endured in a rut no worse than that of many that began as passionate romances and considerably better than many of those in terms of the physical comforts, supportive services, and variety of pleasures that could be purchased. In consideration of the decent fulfillment of his responsibilities, Myron was absorbed peacefully, though not with joy or intimacy, into Edith's family.

## Sex and Money

Their children provide other sources of embarrassment for the rich. Homosexuality has not come so far out of the closet as some of the New York- and San Francisco-based media would have us believe. It is still not unusual for a homosexual person to have to keep up appearances in the family or in a conservative job situation. And some homosexuals want children. So, for whatever reason, he or she marries. Even if there is a great deal of platonic affection and the spouse has agreed to an "arrangement" in advance, it is very difficult for most individuals to live with someone who actively is expressing a sexual preference for someone else. The particular frustration when that preference is homosexual is that the spouse never will have the right physical equipment with which to compete with the lover. Of course, repeated affairs are common in many marriages between heterosexuals, too. If the marriage is to endure, restraint and tact are required. Wealth can make them easier to supply. With large homes, multiple homes and easy travel, more physical space and privacy are available as buffers.

Theoretically, it should be easy for a man or woman who, for various reasons, is not at all interested in the sexual aspect of marriage to find a rich mate who feels the same way and make this common bond the basis of the relationship. Despite an era in which sexual activity is merchandised like vitamins, there are still plenty of people around who are sexually inhibited by fears or realities of illness or by a lifetime of conditioned attitudes. Marriages based on this kind of understanding are made, but the initial discussions require courage. And very often, no matter what agreement has been made, people do not enter such marriages honestly. One or the other really is hoping for a miraculous change. That one tends to resent the partner when it does not happen.

There is also some potential for marriage through sexual rescue, if it really works, and if it is important enough to the "rescued" rich person to endure the various inconveniences that may be involved in formalizing the relationship through marriage. A sexual rescuer might be the first woman who happens to elicit an erection in a man after a period of secondary impotence, the first man to bring a woman to orgasm during intercourse, or the first partner who willingly and satisfactorily indulges a more specialized preference. The risk, of course, is that the rich person may see no need to reward the rescuer with anything so entangling and public as marriage. There are other tokens of appreciation, some quite valuable, that a rich person might find it simpler to bestow. Or he or she may turn out not to be all that grateful, or generous.

## Genius and Celebrity

One thing that appeals to the wealthy who seem to have everything and still are not satisfied is enormous talent or intellect. This tends to attract women more than men, at least in youthful first marriages. Despite some real changes in the past decade, women most often have been brought up to nurture others and to take their identities from the careers of their husbands. So a rich woman may take a chance on marrying and encouraging a young "genius" whose vision has been recognized, but not widely, while rich men tend to be drawn to extraordinarily talented women only after they are famous.

Famous women are more likely to be courted by rich men over fifty who have been married before. Meanwhile, the heiress marries the promising artist/writer/musician/architect. Or the dutiful, brotherless daughter of a powerful father marries the penniless but brilliant young lawyer/engineer/editor/salesman/executive/broker who can become the natural heir to her father's empire. The outcomes vary. Some are successful marriages. Often, no matter how great a personal triumph he has made in Daddy's business, the man feels he has never really proved himself, and the marriage suffers from his self-hatred, expressed as resentment of his wife and father-in-law.

If the woman is a genuine heiress, the couple may use her fortune to start a private school based on his innovative philosophy, publish a new magazine to broadcast his views on social reform, help him run for political office, invest in large-scale building, or found an active new philanthropy. If they both remain interested in the project and appreciative of each other, the marriage may work well.

However, when an heiress marries a promising but poor young man, there are hazards for both. If she has married him more to have someone attractive and compliant to parade around like a pet dog than to nurture his talent, he (when he gets over the dazzle of her wealth and connections) may get tired of the leash and leave. Even with an encouraging wife things can go wrong. He may go sour, become resentful, abuse and humiliate her with insulting behavior, blame her for his failure, have flagrant affairs. Or his talent may simply evaporate in the absence of hard economic challenges.

Consider the example of Ben and Meg. The once-daring lines of the glass-walled house he built for her on the shore of their own little lake have become a worn cliché, but the place is maintained exquisitely, inside and out. Some people can remember that he once got an important award, but no one can remember when he last had a commission. He always says he's busy, researching the feasability of low-cost housing projects using indigenous materials in some out-of-the-way locality, or planning high-density work space on a human scale. No one has seen the plans. Meg has them all filed away, she says, waiting for a change of government regulations or the testing of a new material. No point in doing it if it can't be done right, she says. They travel a lot. At home, Ben presides with an authoritarian air that lapses into boozy pomposity.

Ben is the son of a country parson's daughter and a history professor at an obscure college. Meg's father was an international banker before he became our ambassador to one of the Low Countries. Her mother chaired hospital and museum committees. Meg had exceptional design talent, but women didn't become architects in her day. People whisper about how loyal Meg is, simply pretending not to notice that Ben's early promise has fizzled. She is beginning to get quite a reputation herself for her effective dealings with a rainbow of opposing political factions in the regional planning and zoning battles. Even though she continues to talk about Ben as someone whose work is of importance, she is beginning to enjoy public acknowledgment of her own efforts. Is it possible that whatever disappointment she may feel about Ben is less important than the satisfaction she is getting from being the real achiever in their marriage? Is it possible that Ben's once-ambitious talent has been sandbagged by the perfectionistic cosseting his wife's wealth has allowed?

## New Money

Why the rich marry the non-rich has to do with many minute shadings between contentment and dissatisfaction. The old rich marry out to rebel, to evade competition with parents or siblings, to establish a separate identity, to bolster a dwindling fortune, or to acquire something of value that they don't already possess. The new rich also like to add something of value to their lives through marriage. What this is depends on their specific backgrounds, their individual personalities, the ways in which they have come by their money, the social nature of their ambitions, and on whether they are entering a first or a later marriage.

New money often wants to acquire some form of conspicuously higher social status through marriage. A spouse from the ruling WASP caste represented by such stereotypes as the Boston Brahmins and the Philadelphia Main Line can be particularly desirable to the self-made multimillionaire son of an unskilled laborer. The same WASP socialite, or perhaps any fine-boned, Nordic blonde, may seem to offer an appealing shortcut to a very rich, socially impatient Jew who is not of the old German Jewish aristocracy that has been settled in the United States for four or five generations. The latter, along with a handful of cousins of French descent, often are publicly indistinguishable from the WASP aristocracy. Intermarriage is frequent, though memberships in certain clubs and partnerships in certain firms are still quietly barred. No matter how beautiful black may be, some black male celeb-

rities and their Ivy League-educated sons find that their unusual visibility gives them an option to marry idealistic
daughters of the white elite, and they exercise it. However,
the majority of black men in this country have had little encouragement to move out from an underdog position. So a
bright, well-groomed black professional woman often has a
better chance of marrying a white colleague than a black man
of her own caliber. Many women from a variety of backgrounds who become rich through their own efforts in business or a profession still pine for a man who represents even
more power and achievement.

A socially ambitious, newly rich person chooses a spouse
who can help him demonstrate his eligibility for acceptance
by a particular social group. The mores of the circle to which
he aspires determine the kind of taste, or lack of it, required.
In Meg's parents' house, the possessions of Old Money *look*
old. There is a seventeenth-century Isfahan rug, worn close
to threadbare at an end that no one attempts to conceal. In
the study, a matched set of large, gold-tooled, leather-bound
volumes with crackled, rusty-looking spines is a treasured
eleventh edition of the Encyclopedia Britannica, in use in the
family since 1913. The broad, gleaming partner's desk is an
authentic Georgian masterpiece. Next to it sits a typewriter
on a rickety-looking, drop-leaf metal stand, the latest model
in convenience thirty-five years ago. The Hudson River School
landscape in the drawing room, slightly in need of restora-
tion, is by the dean of the genre, Frederick Church, and was
bought by a great-uncle directly from the artist. No one needs
to look for a signature. To those who belong here, the rare
and valuable things in this house, mixed in among the convenient and practical, need no labels. Recognizing them calls
for a background of familiarity with the history of fine objects
and aristocratic pastimes. Old customs and manners are also
familiar. When, at certain meals, finger bowls are placed on
doilies on each dessert plate, each diner is expected to know

that the doily must be lifted off with the bowl.

The political and moral views of one's companions at that table are also supposed to be known and not challenged. A lively debate about the arms race is welcome, but the latest round of utilities deregulation is not discussed. (Father lost a tidy sum on that one.) Vatican II and Cousin Claire are never mentioned when Uncle Tim is present. (Aunt Mary, for whom he converted, goes only to churches where the old Latin service is used. Their daughter Claire, who campaigned for legal abortion and lives openly with a divorced Italian Communist, has not been in their house in more than a decade.) Conversations on subjects that might evoke family scandals are to be avoided. Restraint and discretion in company are expected.

The less rooted the circle in historic and conservative traditions, the more likely there is to be a display of obviously expensive items and a fascination with costly new gadgets. In Rosalind's and Barbara's circles, the clothing and accessories sport an alphabet soup of designer initials (CD, V, interlocking Gs). Brass bit buckles and breast pocket polo player logos abound. So do materials everyone knows cost a lot. This is marble bathroom and gold faucet country. If the upholstery fabric is from Brunschwig & Fils, Barbara or Rosalind will be sure to tell you so. Conversations include references to the Jacuzzi in the master bath, the Universal equipment in the dressing room, the 733i in the garage, the Jasper Johns at the framer's. All high-status possessions and recognizably high-priced brand names are mentioned. Well-publicized luxury resorts from Las Vegas to Sardinia are chosen for vacations. Cars and clothing get replaced often. The hair style, the VCR and the home computer are likely to be the latest models.

The upper echelons of big city, high status success groups—the Statustocracy—are somewhat more subtle. Samantha and her friends play the game well. It is a ferocious but unspoken competition to be up-to-the-minute with the newest trends in clothing, decor, food, art and gathering places. What's "in" is usually the opposite of what the more obvious *nouveau riche* are buying: white porcelain pedestal sinks instead of marble vanities; plain stripped pine tables instead of glass and steel or fine French; a quiet little inn far from the luxury beach hotels of the Yucatan, reached by a grueling six-hour drive in a Land Rover. The trick is to throw away the references to status labels and to emphasize personal, idiosyncratic choices or refined, practical considerations. "Yes, the sheets *are* Porthault. Nobody else makes pure cotton any more, and I'm allergic to synthetics." "The only reason I drive a Mercedes is that it's the safest car on the road." Some of the choices in these circles, too, can lapse into vulgarity and virtual cloning, but the style is carried off by pretending to take none of it seriously.

For an upwardly mobile man, a beautiful and stylish wife can show off fine clothes and jewels. An accomplished hostess can make the home a memorably enjoyable place in which to be a guest. Knowing which clubs to join, which concerts to attend, which benefits to back with a table or a little dinner at home for eight or twelve or thirty, are important skills on the road to upward mobility. In some circles the wife had better hold her own on the tennis court or at the bridge table. In others, detailed knowledge of the last hundred years of art history is more important. In still others, knowing her place in the hunt field is a requirement, although being a good sport about driving the horse trailer and giving her share of hunt breakfasts might do just as well.

The newly rich man in the Snob Money category wants a wife who will help him blend into the established upper classes as quickly as possible. The Slob Money rich are more inclined to choose someone for purely personal pleasure: a pretty, sexy second wife, a woman who remains demonstrably proud of his achievements, a woman who enjoys the quixotic ways in which he spends money, or a woman who, no matter how much wealth is available, continues to share his respect for the value of a dollar.

Consider Hilda. When she comes into the city, she drives the Bentley around the block twice looking for a parking space before putting it into a garage. Besides the little duplex in town, Hilda and Dan have the mansion in Upper Richdale, the *pied à terre* on the Coast, the beach house in Security Shores, and the condominium in Dinero Sands. The children's wing of the hospital ten blocks away is named for Dan. So is the new gallery of contemporary design at the museum down the street. Dan has set up trust funds for the grandchildren of Hilda's first marriage, as well as for his own. She drives around the block out of habit, and he loves her for it. Her father was an assistant gardener. His father worked on a loading dock. Dan made a staggering pile of money in chemicals and diversified investments, and Hilda married it, but neither of them sees any point in squandering it. Dan learned to find marital contentment the hard way. This time he picked an adaptable woman from a background enough like his own to appreciate his quirks and develop enthusiasm for his interests. His first two marriages were troublesome attempts to move up culturally and socially. This one is bliss.

## What Are You Offering?

Fortunately, the obvious attention getters of beauty, brains and talent are not the only personal traits likely to appeal to a prospective rich mate. For many potential spouses, what appeals to them is whatever makes them feel good. To figure this out in advance, it might help to know the person's parent of the opposite sex and the history of the relationship with that parent. That parent represents the individual's first intense involvement with someone of the opposite sex. Even the total absence of that parent influences later relationships.

A man whose mother died or ran away with a lover when he was a toddler may always keep himself slightly walled off, unable to trust a woman, and may, in unconscious retaliation, always keep several female partners lined up, leaving women before they can leave him. A woman whose father was away a lot or who was completely absorbed in his own interests and indifferent to his little daughter when at home, may always have difficulty finding men who will behave as if they cared for her.

People tend, consciously or unconsciously, to seek in a mate either replicas of qualities they have enjoyed in the parent or the opposites of parental qualities that have caused them pain. However, just which is which is not always obvious. And while expectations based on history with one's parents are subtly pervasive, there are still other forces at work in mate selection. People often seek the opposite of the mistakes they know. If his first wife was a prudish, perpetually dieting housewife who nagged him into an ulcer, it's no surprise that Stan, whose plumbing supply business has become one of the biggest in the county, really goes for Michelle's flashy, plump good looks, her professional career, her easy-going but efficient approach to household management, and her sly suggestion of a mirror on the bedroom ceiling.

If Peter, the heir to a famous but dwindling fortune, decides at thirty-eight that he's ready to settle down and raise a family, the qualities of the wife he chooses will have more to do with integrity and dependability than with the mercurial sexiness of the women he was drawn to at twenty-five. If Wally, the aging boy genius of luxury retailing, had a first wife who could never change her *stetl* habits, his socialite second wife was a bitch on wheels, and his real preference is for men, little blonde Ames's willingness to wear his diamonds and become an expert on gardens and *haute cuisine* and do anything else he tells her is very appealing.

If the well-known novelist over sixty feels depresssed,

with nothing to look forward to, the affectionate attention of a pretty twenty-three year old with an M.A. in literature could be just the thing to revive his spirits and certain physical proclivities. If she can behave well in public, why not reserve her exclusively through marriage? The widower who is isolated and frightened by a long, crippling illness may find the sensitive care of his middle-aged private duty nurse or housekeeper worth rewarding and retaining through marriage. The richer, older spouses in these last two examples could also be women marrying younger caretakers and mood elevators, but social conventions are more tolerant of the reverse May-December situation.

Those who convince a rich man or woman that he or she is admired for the personal characteristics that that individual has always secretly valued most have a head start on a continuing relationship. Most people never can have enough of being appreciated and understood, so long as the appreciator retains credibility. Most people over forty are very much flattered by the romantic and sexual attention of an attractive younger person. By reflection, a sexual liaison with such a person makes them feel younger, more vigorous and attractive themselves. For middle-aged men this age difference can become a key factor in sexual performance. Many literally rise to the challenge, even though a few men in *late* middle age are intimidated by the prospect of performing with a younger woman.

Society condones marriage between younger women and older men. These marriages, with a ten to twenty-five year age span, are common. An attractive, poor, young woman has a much better chance of appealing to a rich, middle-aged man, statistically, than a poor, middle-aged woman does. A middle-aged woman has to use other weapons: wealth of her own, social position and connections of value to that man, extraordinary charm and skill in making him feel understood and appreciated.

While the women's movement has helped to legitimize liaisons between young men and somewhat older women, society as a whole still subjects them to more ridicule than the reverse relationship. However, certain kinds of women are particularly vulnerable to the attentions of attractive younger men. These include women who have been out of circulation for a while. They have been ill, or totally absorbed in business or family responsibilities or only recently have been released from a tie to a man who, because of prolonged physical illness, severe emotional disturbance, or the consequences of an originally dishonest contract, has not shown any affection or sexual attention to them for a long time. Some of these women are rich and willing to share their wealth with a suitor who makes them feel attractive, feminine and sexually desirable.

Sometimes making people feel good is done on a grand scale. In real life, one of the richest men in America, the moody heir to a vast old fortune with no immediate heirs of his own, approached a charming woman shortly after her husband had died. He told her that he had watched her for a long time and admired the extraordinary gift she had for giving people pleasure. He said he would like to think that, after his death, his fortune would be in the hands of someone who would use it for the happiness of others. He asked her to marry him. She accepted. A widow now, she is widely known as a gracious and distinguished philanthropist.

## The Woman Who Makes Money

The successful woman who makes a lot of money represents a growing segment of the newly rich population. While many of these women still seek equally high-powered and even more successful men, they don't always attract or keep them. And another pattern, while not yet widely popular, is emerging. As she approaches forty (if not sooner), the moneymaking female executive/journalist/broadcaster/corporate officer/lawyer/doctor begins to notice that she is lonely. She may have had a disappointing early marriage or some other painful experiences with men in her youth. She has focused ever since on her career and shied away from personal commitment. While she may once have wanted a glamorous man or one more successful than herself, she is now comfortable being the breadwinner and the star. An intelligent, affectionate man with a decent career but one that compared to hers pays modestly (such as college professor, research scientist, public service lawyer), begins to look attractive—provided he is willing to adapt to *her* work schedule, be there to hear about *her* hard day at the office, and take over some of the domestic responsibilities. So long as she really admires him and he respects himself, these marriages can work well.

Many prosperous women over forty are eager for presentable male companionship. On through their fifties and sixties and older, women are guided by the miracles of modern cosmetic science and pop-psych mythology into everlastingly gleaming skin, bouncing bronzed hair and unlimited capacity for orgasm. But they don't find many acceptable male partners available for this promenade of perpetual youthfulness.

## Simple Gifts

Sometimes our value to others takes the form of skills and knowledge we take for granted. A certain assistant professor of literature's most binding link with the rich friends who invite him to dinner regularly is that he can repair any part of a bicycle, and they can do nothing with their hands. I know a woman who can tell you which is the better of two sources in town for quail's eggs and where to go to match your ten-year-old purple towels. While she considers this kind of information essential to her own well-being, it also makes her the treasured friend of several fussy, rich host-esses. Another woman is always invited for weekends when her rich colleague's mother-in-law comes to visit from Quebec, because she is the only person the couple knows who can understand Canadian French. It's a bit of a strain, but eligible single men are also invited to lunch and dinner on those weekends.

The person looking to marry up would do well to ask himself or herself some questions: What bits of skill and knowledge do I take for granted that someone else might value highly? How versatile am I in using the aspects of my personality that fit best in a particular situation? How willing am I to offer what a worthwhile potential spouse needs rather than wait for my ideal admirer to come along?

Pace Dollarson appealed to Mortimer not because she was so beautiful or sexy or brilliant but because she could do something extremely well that he couldn't do at all. He was a morose and self-absorbed man. He didn't know how to give anything but money, and he feared being used for that. Pace could look outward, expend energy on others, address herself to their feelings, their comfort, their pleasure. Mortimer used Pace's personality to supply what he could not.

Dan, the laborer's multimillionaire son who always remembered the value of a dollar, had found the women in his life needy and demanding. While Hilda really liked to be taken care of by a man, she presented herself as interested in taking care of Dan. She made it clear that her business was successful, her life was contented, she didn't need him in order to survive.

Daphne didn't appeal to Phil because of her considerable musical talent. She became indispensable to him because, while he was professionally brilliant, he was socially lazy. She supplied all the effort and organization to keep life going. Samantha didn't appeal to Greg because she sparkled and was competent at many things but because she kept her sparkle subdued enough never to threaten to outshine his own achievement.

Rosalind, groomed to be admired for her dainty prettiness, appealed to Simon because of something else entirely. He never had been able to approach women sexually because he had a fear of hurting them. Rosalind was the first "lady" he had met who was, in private, very aggressive sexually. She relieved Simon of responsibility and guilt. An unabashed climber named Wendy, whose maximum thrust techniques for moving up are described in Chapter 5, projected a smouldering sexuality to most men, but the famous artist who became her most useful stepping stone didn't find her particularly alluring physically. She appealed to this particular man more as a security blanket, providing the tough, shrewd management he needed to cope with the world.

These people all were willing to be valued for whatever appealed most to the other person. These qualities were not necessarily what they liked most about themselves. Can you make a list of everything you have to offer, whether you like it or not? Being able to balance a checkbook, be gracious to stuffy business associates and haughty in-laws, make sure the cars are kept in working order, have the strength to push a wheelchair, keep things going in the face of someone else's massive depression, indecisiveness, sexual inadequacy, bursts of temper, or terror of being alone, these and dozens of other unglamorous abilities may not be what you'd like to advertise about yourself, but one or more of them may be precisely what makes some rich and privileged person want you very much.

## A Natural Enhancement

For many reasons, having money yourself is one of the best ways to have money marry you. Having money doesn't necessarily mean being born with it. It can mean going out and making your own. A person earning a good living and living well evokes less suspicion from a successful potential mate. If both are self-made financially, they have a common basis for respecting each other. Hilda and Dan not only came from parallel backgrounds of immigrant poverty but both had started and run their own businesses. Hilda's was on a modest scale, and Dan's was on a colossal one, but they both were successes. They liked one another's drive.

One of the fringe benefits of making a lot of money can be that it brings the earner into contact with other people who make a lot of money. That depends, of course, on the work setting and how the individual uses the social opportunities it offers. (This will be discussed in Chapter 6.) Making a lot of money may accompany a high prestige occupation or it may put the successful earner in a position to make civic-minded contributions that enhance his or her prestige in the community. That person can also purchase directly more of the pleasures, goods and services of the affluent life. Marriage to an equally affluent or a richer person becomes not a desperate way out but the natural enhancement of an already rewarding life.

People with privileged position marry for the same reasons other people marry: to feel good, to fill a particular need or plan at a particular time, to enhance their lives with something of unique value to them, or to preserve what they already have. Where the marrier-up fits in depends partly on the luck of timing. It also depends on the degree of inclination to be realistic about where he or she is most likely to fill a need.

# 4

## Marriage: Emotional Expectations

### Choice, Chance or Destiny?

*M*any people who say they want to marry claim they never meet anyone. What they usually mean is that no one they meet could be considered a serious candidate. I once overheard a middle-aged saleswoman talking to a friend in the ladies' room at Saks Fifth Avenue. "I've met the man I would marry," she said. "And I've met the man who would marry me, but they weren't the same man."

Our images of marriage and the people we would like to marry get formed from a combination of influences that are not always easy to trace. They come from where we grew up, how the members of our families treated each other, how our individual abilities developed, the range of our social and vocational opportunities, the place of public opinion—and which public?—in our lives. Many people never have a clear idea in advance of the kind of person they would like to marry. They just wait to "fall in love," and that's that. In other words, the selection of a mate is left entirely to unconscious processes.

The deepest unconscious preferences in mate selection

seem to come from patterns associated with a person's earliest experiences of connection with others. If a little boy grows up closely attached to a mother who is depressed and anxious, who teaches him to avoid upsetting her and to look for ways to cheer her, he is likely to be attracted, when he has grown up, to women who, no matter how vivacious their façades, are depressed and anxious. (There is something comfortably familiar about them.) At the same time, he eventually is likely to sniff out, exaggerate and resent the depressed and anxious traits in every woman he meets. A little girl who was adored by a consistently attentive (but not destructively possessive) father will tend to find men in her adult life who show her the same capacity for appreciation and devotion. She will seldom hesitate to drop a man who doesn't. Her history has left her confident that she can always find one who will pay her the proper kind of attention.

Our unconscious preferences include our attempts to compensate for many kinds of losses and injuries. It sounds sinister but it's merely normal. If your earliest experiences have offered a tolerable balance between satisfaction and frustration—weighted somewhat on the side of satisfaction—you have some likelihood of falling in love with a reasonably satisfactory person. If your earliest experiences (I am speaking of infancy and early childhood) have been weighted either toward excessive disappointment and frustration or toward constant, easy gratification, your choices will tend also to be skewed, though not necessarily in a neat, obvious proportion. They could cause you trouble. If you become aware of these directives from your unconscious, you may be able to take charge of deciding whether to act on them or not. You could even learn to make sounder choices. At least you'll understand the kind of trouble you are letting yourself in for.

A banker told me about a holiday weekend spent, through accidents of bad weather and transportation breakdown, with his present and former wives and the children from both marriages. He found it a very enjoyable time. Observing both women together, he was astonished to see how similar they were in appearance, manner and personal preferences. He reported that even though he had not known how to make the first marriage work, and there were some rocky moments in the second, he really liked both women very much. He realized that he consistently chose the same "type" and that it was up to him to accept his predetermined choice and learn how to get along with the actual woman.

## Falling in Love

Love has many forms of expression and undergoes many distortions. Love does not necessarily mean a sexual attachment to another person. There is the altruistic love we feel for a child or any helpless creature who needs our protection and assistance and cannot repay us. There are the respect and admiration and good wishes we might direct to a friend or associate, a blood relative or a teacher, a helper or a public figure. There is the intense enthusiasm to be felt for an endeavor in which we have invested energy and skill. There is self-love, which when it is genuine, enlarges our capacity to love others.

There is another feeling that we sometimes confuse with love. It is an urgent, life-or-death need for constant care and attention from a particular person, preferably to be supplied without our having to ask. This last feeling is appropriate to a very young infant. If the need is not satisfied to some extent, the infant dies or grows up crazy. But in someone old enough to sire or bear infants, basing a sexual or marital relationship primarily on this need creates a distorted set-up destined for trouble. The spouse is blamed too often for not having known or done something without prompting: bought aspirin, sent flowers, called or not called a family member, scheduled an outing or cancelled one. He or she will always be guilty of spending too much time at work or not caring enough about making money, being too gregarious or being too withdrawn, wanting to make love too often or not being amorous enough. The needy spouse will never be satisfied.

Some amount of life-or-death distortion is usually present when people fall in love. Being "in love" is, basically, a demented state in which balanced judgment and objective perception are suspended. This state is often quite agreeable. It's fun to call each other five times a day—for a while. But if the calls become a necessity to ward off panic and rage the fun ceases. The urgent need for reassurance of the partner's total, sympathetic devotion can make being in love painful. However, this demented condition serves to overcome obstacles of logic and convenience that might otherwise stand in the way of marrying. Marriage requires giving up many sensible, selfish comforts available in single life. Instead, one takes on the burdens, frictions and disappointments of life as a couple or a larger family unit. And, at least for a while, one gives up the possibility of meeting a "better" mate. Falling in love to start a marriage is like a political platform: good to get in on, but don't count on it to keep things working.

No marriage can be perfect. Two individuals cannot always have precisely complementary needs or wishes. It is not the absence of disappointment or friction that makes for a good marriage but the proportion of contentment that is there to balance the disappointment. If irritations are handled with respect for the partner, friction can be bearable. It can also give shape to a life. Repeatedly bumping up against another person—metaphorically—becomes a way of defining one's own boundaries.

"The perfect romance" is an illusion that most of us find hard to give up. We always have known or heard of a couple who has lived a perfect romance for twenty or thirty or fifty years. (We also have heard that their children grew up feeling excluded, deficient, resentful, but that's another issue.) Usually, without discussing it, each partner has made a deliberate decision to maintain that illusion of perfect romance. To do so they distort many of their conscious perceptions of each other and of the rest of the world. Of course, any enduring relationship contains elements of these protective distortions. It is a matter of degree.

Many of the women who were raised never to be without a man concoct a one-sided version of the perfect romance. They idealize their husbands, no matter what. One such woman, referring to her "perfect marriage" of twelve years' duration, described with obvious distaste the details of the camping trips her husband had taken her on, yet she insisted that everything about those trips and that her husband was wonderful. When he died, she used this idealization to her advantage. Her next husband was a difficult and ambitious man. She never let a day go by without some apparently innocent reference to her previous "perfect marriage." These reminders helped to keep the new husband's more arrogant tendencies in line. He was competitive enough to want to be considered perfect, too.

## The Only Thing Worse Than Being Married

There is much evidence that although men and women fall in love with each other, they really don't like each other very much. Their upbringing has not trained them to understand each other, but only to assume roles and, nowadays, to discard them. Too many disappointed expectations and too many unwanted responsibilities build walls of resentment and suspicion.

In the *How To Marry Money* classes and in my psychotherapy practice, when I ask men or women what they are looking for in a marital partner, I am most likely to hear first what they don't want. Men complain about self-absorbed women wrapped up in their own successes, snobbish about the men's career status, socially and sexually demanding. But if the woman is hesitant and uncertain about her job and other choices, he's just as likely to criticize her for being childish, passive and without direction. Women complain that men don't want to get involved, they're selfish and inattentive and often they are sexually unsatisfactory. Or they are too possessive and not sympathetic to the demands of her career.

More than one man in the *How To Marry Money* classes has said that if he were to marry a rich woman, he would want her to be an heiress rather than a successful professional woman, because he would want a wife to be loving and attentive and sympathetic to him. He wouldn't expect to get this from a woman whose biggest priority is her job. In several classes successful women executives, always gorgeously groomed, have complained about the men they meet. The story is usually the same. They don't call her enough. They don't take her to good restaurants. They don't give presents. They don't suggest going anywhere. This is not a woman earning fifty-nine cents on the male dollar. She is in, or getting close to, the six-digit bracket. But she usually is appalled when I ask if she ever has offered a good example herself of what she wants from men. Does she ever invite a man to dinner at a smart restaurant, order fifth-row center theater tickets, give him an appropriately amusing birthday present?

Despite these complaints, my daily newspaper is full of wedding and engagement announcements. In most of them both the bride and the groom are described as engaged in responsible, paying occupations. In my office I see the conflicts with which some of these couples struggle. At work the women are caught up in competitive achievement. They enjoy being the knight who slays the dragon. In personal life they still long to be the maiden who gets carried off on the white horse. Liberated from the vocational and sexual restraints of their parents' generation, they assume that they are supposed to have everything. They send out a lot of conflicting signals.

The men are confused and wary. They don't know how to read the signals. They can't tell if they are talking to a playmate or a competitor. They are hurt. Men don't have the training women do in accepting their own vulnerability. It may have to do with their anatomy. Sexually, men are more vulnerable than women, more exposed, not able to hide very easily. The tough, aggressive stance they have been taught is largely a defense. They can learn to live comfortably with uncertainty and confusion, but only if they are given some evidence that they are not going to be kicked where it hurts most every time they let those old defenses down.

While occasional periods of solitude can be refreshing, most people do not function well in prolonged isolation. Vows of silence and solitary existences among the religious are feats of discipline and faith, sustained by belief in a higher being and a spiritual community. Out in the everyday world, people do need other people. We think of women as being conditioned to build their lives around a man, a conditioning many have tried to shake with varying success. But men depend more than we realize on the presence of a woman to define them as lovers and providers and human beings. Sooner or later most people want that feeling of continuity, the knowledge that someone is there, the extra charge and the resilience that come with caring for someone other than oneself. Despite its flaws and its frictions, marriage remains a possible structure for these things.

Even when it fails miserably, marriage is missed. Even when it represents the frightening unknown, it still appeals. A woman may have been the steady provider and manager while her husband zigzagged through shabby schemes and philandering, but when they separate, to her surprise, she feels shaky and unprotected. A young man decides to marry his demanding, temperamental girlfriend rather than remain alone or risk getting stuck with someone worse. Marriages laced with tension and fury continue for years because for many people, the only thing worse than being married is not being married.

## The Right Fit

Marriage provides a structure for relationships. Even in the present period of shifting roles and reassigning tasks, marriage helps people to define their loyalties and responsibilities. Marriage also helps to define a person to the world. A senator's husband, an alcoholic's wife, a tycoon's widow, are "placed" in relation to the spouse.

Sometimes love evolves for a person you were not particularly thrilled to meet. But that person turns up and starts treating you the way you always wanted to be treated. When the wish to marry up to the amount of money or the kind of position to which you feel entitled is added to the wish for love, there is an even greater need to adjust the fantasy to the available reality. Usually the fantasy is to add a charming, intelligent, attractive, witty, loving, devoted, well-connected spouse to whatever else you currently enjoy in life. There are such people, but why would they want you?

Sometimes people have to look at themselves clearly in the mirrors—inner and outer—assess what they have to offer and then decide what matters most to them among all that they think they want. That was the case with Francine. She was the clever, witty, ugly duckling. Middle aged, middle class and never married, she felt without identity outside her academic career. In a man she had always sought glamour, status, fashionable intellect, social connections. Without realizing it she hoped to find in a man the image of everything she wanted to be herself. She could look at him as in a mirror and be pleased with herself. In her youth she had found such men to borrow occasionally, but never to keep.

She began to feel so lonely and unlovable that she thought about suicide. Instead she invested some time and money in exploring her feelings and their causes, with professional help. She came to terms with a great many facts about herself: her charm and its limitations, her background and the boundaries of its appeal. What she needed most from a man was affection, compatibility, dependability, not glamour. She would even be willing to let her career slip a little if she found those things.

Six months after making this decision she met George. He was widowed, a careful man, successful in a small manufacturing business and some real estate investments, without social distinction. He was delighted to look to Francine for spontaneity and the whiff of intellectual elegance that the style of her professional associations brought to his routine comforts. When people are attracted to each other, they believe they see in the other person something they want to enhance their lives. This time, Francine wanted what she really needed, and she found it in someone who wanted what she really had to offer.

Sometimes the fit of a couple's needs is not so comfortable. Wally, the luxury retailer who found wives a necessary evil, turned up some pages back with pretty little Ames. She had been Amy, the fourth grade teacher's daughter, growing up in Ohio, but in New York, she noticed from following the society pages that the most pampered rich women had tough, one-syllable names. These were parts of family names or epithets from boarding school hockey fields mellowed into nicknames. Ames was her own idea. Too short for high fashion modeling, she worked in showrooms and talked about taking classes and becoming a designer. She married Wally instead. He already had achieved everything she could dream of professionally. She was nervous but willing to help with the social side.

Ames presided at Wally's store openings and promotional extravaganzas, as well as in their several living rooms filled with a mixture of chic contemporary design and rare antiques. She went to the right exercise class and sat with the right ladies at the fashion shows. She bore the obligatory child and sent it to the right schools, where Ames made friends with the right mothers. (The child is obligatory for its mother's financial protection and for its father's self-image.) Ames was helping Wally reach new rungs on the social ladder, but alone at home he scorned her conversation and addressed her like a servant. After the child was produced, Wally and Ames' sex life ceased. He traveled on business a lot with his male assistant and left Ames home.

When the hairdressers and the gourmet cooking classes and all the other ladies' activities could not fill the gaps, and an affair was too risky because Wally was capable of having her followed, alcohol and depression took over. With Ames in that condition, Wally's treatment of her went from bad to brutal. She spent a little time in drying out hospitals and a lot more in spas that specialize in the watchful pampering of rich women who cannot stay weaned from the bottle. Ames thought about leaving Wally. She decided to stay until the child was in college. By then, she realized she had no place to go and no way to live. A fate of loneliness in luxurious surroundings was not the worst she could imagine, so she put the lid on her store of wounded feelings and crushed expectations and determined to stay. She always managed to look wonderful at charity balls and other public events.

Francine's marriage was an intelligent decision enhanced by affection. Ames' marriage was a shaky investment in glamour and financial ease. Other people make other kinds of marital investments. Living in the middle of a nasty little tale, or a nice one, may not feel the same as looking at it from the outside. What looks like hell on earth to you or me may be quite comfortable for its inhabitants. What we view as enviable may spell unmitigated misery to its possessor.

## Big Leaps Versus Small Steps

Among the most dramatic examples of big leaps up in the world are the Eva Perons and her soulmates everywhere. These are the women who have used sexual liaisons ruthlessly as stepping stones to the top. In or out of marriage, the usual technique is not to let go of the current man until the next one is firmly committed and available. There are women currently admired in public for their independence but whose earliest moves up were achieved in the same way as Evita's.

Whether the marrier-up is a woman or a man, rags-to-riches marriages seldom turn out well. Many times, climbs to the financial and social top through sequential marriages up seem to fare better in terms of endurance. Drue Heinz, Mary Lou Whitney, Gloria Guinness were women who made it on looks, charm and sex appeal and stayed married to the richest of their several husbands. According to Sheilah Graham, in *How to Marry Super-Rich*, Drue Heinz, wife of the 57 Varieties magnate with a fortune in the hundreds of millions, started out scrimping along stylishly on modest means in England. Mary Lou Whitney, wife of Cornelius Vanderbilt Whitney, twenty-seven years her senior, was the daughter of a butcher. She worked in a drugstore in Kansas City before starting out for the big time. Gloria Guinness, wife of a merchant banker who inherited two hundred million dollars, began life in a back street in Vera Cruz, Mexico, daughter of a seamstress or milliner. Each of these women started from a lesser economic level and acclimatized herself to higher standards of living through several marriages that represented interim moves up. But these spectacular climbs are extremely risky and out of reach of most people, even those who have excellent potential for some kind of upward mobility.

In the sensational 1982 Pulitzer divorce, a penniless wife's sexual infidelities were used by the wealthy and far from innocent husband as ammunition to deprive her of child custody as well as of substantial alimony. The widely publicized event provided an exception to the usual pattern for women's top-of-the-heap marriages. These generally have had better staying power than those of their climbing male counterparts. Perhaps this is so because women usually are more adaptable socially. Perhaps it is so because the financially poorer women, with fewer options in life, have been more willing to tolerate difficult behavior and repeated extramarital sexual liaisons on the parts of their richer husbands than the rich women are willing to tolerate on the part of their poor husbands.

Even though Americans are traditionally mobile, most people have a limited amount of tolerance for the degree of difference they can cope with in any given period. Even though we can buy tools and services to help us adapt to change— cultural tutors, speech teachers, wardrobe consultants, financial advisers and psychotherapists to deal with the emotional impact—our preferences and capacities have pretty well been shaped by early, repeated influences in our lives. We are all most comfortable dealing with what we know and are easily disoriented by the unfamiliar and unexpected. Often, people who think about marrying vast wealth or powerful social position don't really want to take a chance on trying to do it. For most of the people who really do want to marry up, moving up just a little through marriage is the most realistic and comfortable goal. It usually leads to a more satisfactory outcome for both partners.

## And They Lived Happily Ever After

Marriage may represent an economic and social move up, but it is also a relationship with another human being. If the quality of life after moving up is to be worthwhile, it is essential that the potential marrier-up also think seriously about his or her preferences in people. With whom can he or she tolerate—preferably enjoy—living? Personality, background, education, interests, attitudes, life goals and personal habits must figure in anyone's fantasies about life with another person.

One way for an individual to start exploring this kind of fantasy is to make some lists. One list would consist of the *qualities considered desirable* in a potential mate. The possibilities are as diverse as individual human personalities, but a starter selection might be made from some of the following:

Kindness
Integrity
Sense of humor
Steel trap mind
Beautiful body
Taste for adventure
Capacity for quiet coziness

Another list would be more elaborate, an outline of the *kind of life it would be desirable to share*. This list might consider items along the following lines:

Intellectual and moral values
Political, cultural and recreational preferences
Involvement in community activities
Time required by each spouse for privacy or separate
    interests
Amount of attention required by each spouse
Compatability of careers
Feelings about children, including presence of children
    from a previous marriage
Nature of relationships with in-laws or other extended
    family

A third list would name the *characteristics and conditions that would make life intolerable enough to rule out a potential spouse.*

Daphne, as determined as she was to move up in the world, would not have married a man who exhibited a bent for philandering or other reckless adventures, no matter how great his wealth. For her the security she sought depended on a stable home, as well as on money and social position. Hilda's husband, Dan, the penny-pinching, self-made multimillionaire, divorced his previous wives in large part because he could not live with a woman who would not devote herself primarily to his concerns. Samantha could not have settled in with a man whose life was comfortable but routine, without the excitement of bold new ventures and public attention. Some disqualifying characteristics from their combined lists would read as follows:

Infidelity
Recklessness
Self-absorption
Lack of attention
Dull routine
Low profile

Still a fourth list might speculate on the *circumstances under which conditions once thought to be intolerable might become bearable, or even welcome*

What things would make a person desirable in spite of irritating habits, unresolved disagreements and thwarted plans?
What serendipitous factors could alter tastes and preferences?
When could great sex or pots of money or recognition by taxi drivers and headwaiters make such things as bedridden depressions, shady stock manipulations, or habitual flatulence cute little quirks instead of major offenses?
How much money for private spaces and household services would change the prospect of children from a de-

manding, noisy, intrusive restriction into an agreeable bonus?

How much creative talent and uplifting goals would be required to compensate for a severely self-centered and overbearing manner?

Fortunately for the process of pairing off, each individual's requirements are enormously different and are subject to change over time. One woman's hunk is another woman's bore; one man's shrew becomes another's cherished protector.

## Life is Not Fair

There are widows living high up behind the multiple security systems of Sutton Place South and Lake Shore Drive and South Ocean Drive, pointing out to visitors their views of boats or bridges or sunsets or city skylines, who started life struggling behind the counters of mom and pop candy stores. There are others who started out in the candy store and are ending their days in cramped rooms of Health Related Facilities overlooking the forlorn winter beaches of the never fashionable Rockaways. What is the difference between them? Why did one move up to a world of security and the other not quite manage to gain a toehold on comfort?

Frequently we find clues in individual histories, differences in aptitude, application or shrewdness. Sometimes the answer lies in a story Carl Sandburg used to tell. (The longest version is in his *Home Front Memo*.) Two maggots fell off a ditch digger's shovel. One landed in a barren crack in the sidewalk and starved. The other landed in a maggot jackpot, a pile of dead rats. He grew fat and sleek. He leaned over toward his dying former companion and shouted, "I owe it all to brains and personality!" The neighborhood around one candy store might have deteriorated into a dangerous ghetto.

The other store may have occupied the last piece of land in a parcel being assembled for an office skyscraper.

Even among the fortunate, there are gradations based on the luck of the draw, where you fell off the shovel, out of whose womb you emerged. Cal Bucksborn and Doug Middleworth were classmates at prep school and friends on the swimming team at Dartmouth or Stanford or Duke. Their grades were equally satisfactory. They were both good-looking, well-mannered and popular. After college Doug went on for an M.B.A. at Wharton. Cal went to work for his father, who was president of Amalgamated Production Diversified. The stock is wholly owned by the family. Doug's father was a branch office manager for a large insurance company. His grandfather had been a stockbroker before the 1929 crash.

Thirteen years later, Doug has just been made a vice president at the advertising agency to which he had returned after several moves, including a stint in a major client's marketing department. He is living in an eight-year-old builder's contemporary with a cathedral ceilinged living room and nice trees in a suburb chosen partly for its excellent public schools and partly for its tolerable commuter transportation. He may put in a swimming pool next year. Someone comes in once a week to help with the heavy cleaning. Suzanne, Doug's wife, used to work in television production. They met on the set of a commercial. She is planning to open a kitchen boutique when the youngest child starts first grade. Doug and Suzanne usually manage a week by themselves in Antigua in February, if Suzanne's mother feels well enough to come and look after the kids. In August, the Middleworths rent a house at a quiet beach where their neighbors are college professors and psychoanalysts.

Cal is living on a different scale. When his father steps up and creates the job of chairman next year, Cal will become president of A.P.D. He and Betts live in town and have a country house within weekend commuting distance. The children's horses are there. The caretaker, an artist whose wife teaches in a private school, looks after things in exchange for a small salary and a rent-free cottage. Cal and Betts have a daily housekeeper and hire caterers for parties, but their only live-in staff is the "baby sitter," whom they will keep until the youngest child is in boarding school. Cal and Betts go out a lot in the evening. His aunt's house in St. Barts is available for long weekends. Sometimes they combine his business trips to Brussels and Frankfurt with excursions to favorite four-star restaurants in France. Flying on the Concorde gives them extra time in Europe.

Betts is on the board of a family service agency and is active in party politics. She has a masters degree in political science and has worked on the planning board. She has a "tiny" trust fund from her grandmother. She would accept a full-time appointment at the state or city level. Betts roomed with Cal's cousin at Vassar. In the summer before her senior year, she met Cal when his cousin brought him to her family's "camp" in the Adirondacks.

Even though Cal and Doug work in the same city, they seldom meet now. Neither made a decision to drop the other. What each could afford had a lot to do with the different habits they evolved. Doug is not unfamiliar with the quietly elegant restaurants where Cal is well-known at dinnertime, but for Doug, they are only places to take a top client occasionally for an expense account lunch. Cal usually lunches in his office dining room, sometimes plays squash at his club at lunch time. Suzanne and Betts are cordial, but conversation falters after the questions about the children. Their frames of reference are so different. Suzanne's clothes tend to be slightly more stylish, but Betts' are of impeccable quality: cashmere, linen, pure silk, polished calfskin, and no designer initials. The buttons on the cuffs of Cal's custom-tailored jackets emerge from finely-stitched, handmade buttonholes. Doug would find it embarrassing to admit to Cal that he never has been on the Concorde. For Cal, bent on convenience, the extra thousand dollars or so in fare doesn't matter that much.

Throughout their school years, Cal's and Doug's potential appeared pretty much the same. Today Doug would not be considered poor by anyone's standards. But he will never catch up with the head start provided by Cal's family business. If Doug had been exceptionally brilliant and driven to make his mark professionally, no matter what the cost to his personal life, his story might have been quite different. He might have aimed for top academic standing and awards. He might have put in sixteen hours every day at innovative ventures and attracted backers. But Doug and Cal represent men of ordinary intelligence, with better than average educational and career opportunities, normally hardworking habits, and the capacity to enjoy the relationships that fall naturally within their reach.

If Doug had let his business mind, rather than other considerations, guide him in choosing the women he dated, he might have made a better match, financially speaking, and found himself closer to Cal's position. If Doug and Suzanne were to divorce within the next ten or fifteen years, he could, if he wished, find a well-off widow or divorcee or successful professional woman to marry and raise his standard of living.

However, at forty-five or fifty, Doug, like most of his peers, probably would prefer to bolster his own illusion of youth by reflecting it more authentically in a woman under thirty. Suzanne's most likely prospects at that point would be a single father seeking help with his children, a much older man, or a young man who wanted to be taken care of. If her boutique were to become successful, she could supply that care on several levels.

## For Better or For Worse

There are social and business advantages to being part of a couple. Most people over thirty are married. Most people are comfortable associating with those similar enough to themselves to reaffirm the rightness of their choices. A person who remains single is a mystery, a challenge to marriage in general if he or she seems contented, or a challenge to a particular couple if he or she is especially attractive or attentive. A married person is often subject to less speculation and scrutiny, is simply accepted as "normal" and "safe."

Some of the conditions that people name as reasons to marry are acquired in marriage: responsible companionship; continuity of shared experience; the security that comes from knowing someone else is there and does care; affection that transcends passion and survives compromise. The structure of marriage offers boundaries and friction that we often need in order to understand ourselves and use ourselves well. It offers the opportunity to stretch beyond self-absorption. Families can be Towers of Babel, but there is also great potential for cooperative functioning in family life. These are all workable reasons to marry.

But much of what people say they want through marriage, particularly the people who say they want to marry up, is available in other ways. There is no reason to wait for marriage in order to achieve the income and respect that come from having a good job and the training necessary to get it. Or a place in a community. Or some planning for financial security. These are things anyone can work on now, even if times are hard and life is difficult. Even if it means working two jobs, going to school at night, getting help from people one doesn't like. Finding interests, joining organizations and activities, overcoming shyness and laziness, exploring things beyond the first frustration or disappointment. If you can't do these things for yourself, you probably are looking for impossible miracles from marriage. You probably are concentrating on unworkable reasons to marry.

Like money, marriage is not a cure-all. Entered wisely, it can enhance the life of an already confident and capable person. It seldom saves the life of a frightened and floundering one. Marriage will not correct your poor opinion of yourself. Marriage will not let you escape permanently from the world and its competition. Protective husbands tire of shrinking violets, cheat on them, abuse and discard them. Protective wives get fed up even sooner, unless they need the weak husband to bolster their own shaky self-esteem. Then they have nagging, deprecating ways of making the husband feel miserable in the process.

Many women, like Ames, clutch at success or achievement by association through marriage. They really want recognition of their very own, but they fear that they can't compete and win it for themselves. Many men fall in love disastrously with the same woman over and over. She appears compliant, attentive, concerned only with his needs. He is always surprised later at how rigid and demanding she turns out to be. All these unworkable reasons for marrying at every economic level add more than a touch of desperation to the desire for a spouse who represents a move up. They certainly do not make that spouse more attainable, or more bearable.

## Money, Love and Marriage

Understood properly, money, love and marriage all can serve as buffers in dealing with life's raw curves. Money is an instrument for obtaining some of what we value or need to survive. Love is an emotion without which not much in life seems worthwhile. Marriage is a structure for defining and preserving relationships. We can aim for one or two or all three. Aiming successfully requires that we explore the world around us, as well as our own selves. It requires naming specific goals that lie within the realm of realistic possibility and then determining what we are willing to do to work toward them.

If marrying up is a serious goal, forget the dream of immediate leisure and luxury. The next eight chapters offer suggestions, but no list of ten places to plunk yourself down and have the rich singles fall all over you. There are many examples, a few probabilities, but no simple formulas and no guarantees. Instead, there are guidelines for assessment, clues to resources and illustrations of strategies. There is room for response to the happy accident, but an ambitious goal most often requires work and discipline, risk and compromise, and certain kinds of sacrifice.

# Part II

# Resources

## Exploring the options

In the fields of observation, chance favors
only the mind that is prepared.

Louis Pasteur

# 5

## Meeting Money and Other Kinds of Wealth

### Where to Look

In order to marry up, to money or one of its equivalents, you have to meet it. Some people stumble across money by accident while looking for star billing or a cure for the common cold or the perfect suntan. Samantha stumbled on privilege and prestige while looking for people who were stimulating, purposeful and fun to be around. Myron stumbled on money while pursuing a career that represented a retreat from commercial and social pressures. However, a person who has set the goal of marrying up can't depend on accidents. The marrier-up needs to know the most likely places to meet "money" and how to recognize it when met. He or she needs to know who inherits money and who makes money, where they work and how they spend their time away from work. It is necessary to know what they look like, what they sound like, and how to sort out the skillful pretender from the real thing. These are the resources in the field of marrying up.

It is easy to find entertaining and informative reading on the very rich. Stephen Birmingham and Cleveland Amory, among others, have traced the histories of the German Jews, the lace-curtain Irish, the Boston Brahmins, the descendants of the robber barons and other American dynasties of money and power. There are books about families of wealth and fame on the scale of the Rockefellers, the Dodges, the Vanderbilts. Periodically, magazines such as *Fortune, Forbes,* and the news weeklies feature articles listing many of the richest individuals and families in America, giving ages, geographic locations, and informed estimates on the sizes and the sources of their fortunes. They point out how difficult it is to be specific about wealth when a person is among those three or four hundred whose individual holdings are worth over a hundred million dollars. They remind us that the life styles of these individuals are often no different from those of people in the five to ten million dollar category. They describe these life styles, and they name names.

It never hurts to recognize an important name or a wealthy connection. It is useful to be informed on a subject that is of some interest everywhere, even if only as the lightest or most deprecating form of gossip, in the circles in which one hopes to travel. However, despite the historical examples of Anne-Marie and Bobo, Drue and Mary Lou, and the six husbands of Woolworth heiress Barbara Hutton, most people interested in marrying up are not going to make it into the two hundred million or into the five million dollar class. Many would be delighted to reach Doug Middleworth's options or Daphne's degree of middle American affluence. At that level the names of those with money, or the potential for making it, are not listed directly in books and magazines. The clues to this kind of upward mobility are varied and subtle. Access to it can come about in dozens of different ways.

## The Pebble in the Pool

Setting out to find a mate with money—or any mate at all—is not like aiming one arrow straight at a clearly marked target. (In case you never noticed, even Cupid is usually pictured with a good supply of arrows in that sheath slung over his shoulder.) It is more a process of dropping a pebble in a pool, or many pebbles in many pools. Each time, the pebble sets off a series of quickly expanding rings that skim the surface in wider and wider circles. If the goal is to meet one person richer than oneself to marry, the best chance lies in putting oneself in a position to meet many people who are richer. The idea is to expand all one's circles of acquaintance, with upward mobility in mind. Instead of focusing entirely on meeting that one person with money to marry, the marrier-up allows for the opportunity of an appropriate mate to emerge from the wider and more affluent circles in which he or she becomes accustomed to spending his or her time.

Remember how Daphne was taught to make friends with the rich kids in school? No husband turned up there, but she picked up information and customs very useful in her upward climb. Then she set out deliberately to find a job in an environment where potentially successful men were trained. If she had not connected with Philip or another husband within three years there, she would have looked for new circles in which to pursue her goal. She would have changed her job. She might have relocated, but only to a neighborhood associated with wealth and refinement, even if she lived there in an attic room. She would have become an active member of a prestigious church. She would have joined any organization she could have gotten into that was run and frequented by people of established affluence. She would have remained very much involved in the alumni affairs of her prestigious college.

For those who did not get as early a start as Daphne, it still is possible to catch up. The latecomer to marrying up will need to examine all the ways he or she spends time and consider how these same hours could be refocused to put his or her circle of acquaintance in step with his or her goals. If you are serious about moving up it becomes important to look at everything you do, every place where you can be found, in terms of the opportunities they offer for establishing a network to further your ambition. No matter what other value they have in your life (and I sincerely hope they do), you must look at your friends, acquaintances, colleagues— everyone you deal with—in terms of their potential for being of use in your plan for upward mobility. The workplace, the neighborhood, the special project or cause, the places where you shop, relax, take care of your body, nourish your mind, how you travel between the places you frequent, any form of experience that offers repeated contact with a particular group of human beings, has some potential for establishing a network.

Building a network means making friends, not just finding lovers. It is possible to make friends with members of the opposite sex, of course (the trick is to be sexually appealing without being sexually available), but it is essential to make friends with people of the same sex and with married couples. When people are accustomed enough to a newcomer to treat him or her as one of them, they are more inclined to share information about additional people in the common circle and in their other circles. Trading information is one of the most important functions of a network. When through their networks, movers-up are exposed to individuals or couples who have had a chance to get to like them or find them useful, there is some possibility that the new acquaintances will include the movers-up in more of their activities and introduce them to other people they know.

The mover-up must participate actively, must recognize opportunities and use them. The mover-up is always willing to come along to a prestigious address to which he or she has not been invited before. At the party, the gourmet take-out shop, the committee meeting, the dermatologist's waiting room or the club's hot tub, the mover-up never begrudges five minutes' conversation with a person he or she has not met before, no matter what the age, sex, or overall appeal of the person. That five minutes is spent gathering as much data as possible on the person's connections, activities and locus operandi. Some of the contacts made in this way will lead to entirely different circles and the start of new networks. For the movers-up who participate actively, the networks keep on expanding.

## Gilt by Association

A network can also function to enhance an individual's image in the eyes of people who meet him or her for the first time. In meeting and assessing other people no one has pure, untinted, twenty-twenty vision. We carry our histories with us and when we meet someone new, what we see is determined to some extent by what we have experienced before in similar situations or with people who are superficially similar. The new person might have the same physique, speak in the same accent, do the same kind of work as someone who pleased us or disappointed us in the past. Before we have exchanged two sentences, we have a certain set of expectations.

Our perceptions are also influenced by the surroundings in which we meet a person. An unkempt young man with a low-key, breezy manner may seem charming and aristocratic if he is met lounging against a foreign sportscar parked near the swimming pool at the country home of the distinguished couple we know to be his parents. The same young man may seem sinister if he is encountered lounging against a souped-up Dodge parked near a laundromat in a neighborhood of subsidized housing projects. A thirty-five year old woman made up dramatically and poured into a shiny jumpsuit may strike the observer as cheap and desperate if observed in a public singles disco. But the same woman in the same outfit may seem elegant and stunning if she is presiding at a cocktail party filled with stars of the art and fashion worlds in her own duplex penthouse.

You may be conservatively well-dressed, courteous, amusing and well-spoken, but you are likely to give a different impression to someone who meets you in the lobby of a convention hotel than to someone who meets you as a fellow dinner guest in the well-appointed mansion of the Van Lucre family. If you are identified with a status that the other person values, you are more desirable. You are more likely to be addressed and listened to, remembered and treated with respect.

We like to think that ability and hard work conquer all. They often can, but there are other things that give some people head starts. If two talented, wispy young actresses with fuzzy voices audition well for the same part, why shouldn't it tip the balance if the director knows that one of them is the daughter of a famous theatrical couple? It isn't only the starting salary that makes a young law school graduate pleased to say he works for Cravath, Swaine and Moore in New York City rather than for Finklestein, Murphy and Pellegrino in Nowhere, Nebraska. The Wall Street firm's name conjures up immediate connections to power, big estates, large corporations, government advisers, the status by association that the young lawyer will enjoy even if he never becomes a partner or deals directly with a client. It's the associations that matter when a suburban couple insists on making it clear that they live in Grosse Pointe Farms, and not simply Grosse Pointe.

This claiming of high status associations is sometimes an attempt to feel acceptable to oneself. But very often it is a realistic appraisal of what it takes to be initially acceptable to others. It's that first, superficial recognition that opens the doors and gives a person's other qualities a chance to shine.

A man or woman may be attracted to someone very different for a fling. Certain "foreign" characteristics and novel points of view can be refreshing and challenging for periods of time. But for a sustained relationship, most individuals are more comfortable if the refreshing "foreigner" turns out to speak the same language. That is, the "poor foreigner" must accept the customs and share the values of the "rich native." A new arrival's familiarity with more affluent ways of doing things allows the rich and successful to be comfortable with the newcomer.

## The Lone Wolf and the Lonely Prey

When an individual is introduced through a circle of re-spected mutual acquaintances or in a way that establishes certain high status associations, that individual may be treated better than if met as an isolated stranger. Men and women sometimes do connect through chance meetings in unfamiliar situations. Occasionally they marry and stay together com-fortably. More often they have brief affairs. Many people go away to places where they are not known in order to drop the constraints of their daily lives and find out what it feels like to be wild and free. "Going away" may be to a foreign country, to a different town, or to a bar in a distant neigh-borhood frequented by people one is not likely to meet any-where else. Being wild and free may come down to abdicating any sense of responsibility toward the people one meets, using another person for the pleasure of the moment, and leaving. Sometimes the using is mutual and pleasurable. Often, one person gets hurt.

There is no guarantee that someone introduced as an habitué in the best of circles won't get hurt by one of its members. However, respected, continuing connections offer more inducement to behave well and less pressure to get intensely involved quickly. A network can offer access to other sources of information about a newly met person and can serve as a cautious balance or as support for an individual's impressions. People who meet from time to time in such circles have a chance to get to know each other without haste and to find out whether or not they really might care for each other. They have the freedom to decide to remain simply acquaintances. They can keep other options open for the future. Unpressured time also allows people to get used to what they don't like about each other. If the undesirable features are experienced in overall perspective, after a while, they may turn out to be scarcely noticeable. Many a frog has turned into a prince as circumstances allowed his kindness or wisdom, strength or generosity to reveal itself. The one-shot meeting doesn't give a potential partner that opportunity.

There are many clever suggestions in circulation for gaining one-shot exposure to affluent members of the opposite sex. Some of these sound like locker room bravado. Others might be useful, not directly for meeting a future mate, but generally as part of the upgrading of an operating environment, and only for someone who can afford them without sacrificing more important things. Suggestions include subscribing to a luxury commutation service, such as a helicopter to the Hamptons, frequenting the barbers and hairdressers, the doctors and dentists, the food stores, the veterinarians and pet grooming services and, if you can get into them, the gyms and health clubs patronized by the rich. In case you can't join the right club, I actually have heard it suggested that you commute some distance to do your morning jogging in a neighborhood where rich people jog. Of course most of the people you meet will be married or gay, as will most of the people you meet in any affluent location (the proportions vary according to locality). However, these strategies might offer some long-shot opportunities for adding to your networks if you are friendly, aggressive, and attractive but not too attractive to socialize with a married couple without becoming a threat.

There are other suggestions that I find more distressing

in their passivity and tones of desperation. One in this category is to make a first-class plane reservation which you
keep cancelling at the last minute. You use the ticket as entree
to hang around the first-class lounge and see who is there to
be met. Another is to book yourself into a hotel on a weekend
when you know there will be a convention of high-status,
high-income professionals. One problem with these strategies is that they require a large cash investment. Another is
the implication that you really don't have much to do with
your time. If that is so, how interesting a person could you
be to meet? Another difficulty is that, even if you do find a
handsome plastic surgeon or a beautiful radiologist, that person may be available only for a weekend fling.

These odds are no worse than at any resort or bar on the
singles scene. One of the problems with the singles scene is
that you only get one chance to connect with a person before
he or she disappears forever. Some people are so extraordinary—so striking to look at, so brilliant, so fantastically
good in bed or so completely the image of the other's fantasies—that one meeting is enough to get them pursued to
the ends of the earth. But such people don't need suggestions
on how to meet someone. The first three qualities are combinations of natural attributes and acquired skills. The fourth
is one of those accidents that can't be planned or taught.

## Matchmaking

Most big cities have several kinds of commercial matchmaking services available. The idea makes sense, but in use,
the climate of urgency and the gaps in the subscribers' self-
esteem can keep these services from working out successfully. The really rich and well-connected don't use these services. The striving, upwardly mobile sometimes do.

For most Americans formal, paid matchmaking feels like
a haphazard and embarrassing enterprise. It can be done

through personal ads: w.m. 37, professional, dependable, short, likes baroque music and gourmet tours, seeks educated, well-groomed petite w.f. 23–30 with compatible interests for long-term relationship. Or it can be a sophisticated, computerized service in which applicants get videotaped previews before deciding to request an introduction. These methods, even when they lead to meeting someone seriously interested in matrimony and technically suitable, are subject to the membership syndrome described by several generations of American humorists: I wouldn't want to belong to the kind of club that would accept me as a member.

In the matchmaking situation, the feeling that "there must be something wrong with me" gets projected onto the other person: What's wrong with him or her to have to resort to this method of meeting someone? A meeting arranged through a paid service, even more than a blind date arranged through a friend, has a tendency to put both people on trial. The dialogue is a series of booby-trapped tests. The major focus is the other person's flaws, and the flaws can end up being all that is seen. A person who might be appealing in other circumstances gets rejected in this kind of strained evaluation. If not enough flaws are obvious, terrible things are imagined: he's a psychotic sex maniac; she has herpes and won't tell me; his business must be a Mafia front; she's looking for somebody to support her parents. Or there are worries about oneself: I must have bad breath; I have nothing to say; I'm a failure; everybody hates me, just let me out of here. A little self-confidence and a little genuine curiosity about the other person could ease the situation, but the pressure to make an immediate decision is too urgent. The usual solution is to flee.

Most people need more frequent exposure under less pressured circumstances in order to allow their own best qualities to shine and in order to discover the things that really are appealing about someone else. So we return to the building of networks, those circles of upwardly mobile contacts to be developed through work, family, school, recreation, organizations and special interests, to give anyone who wants them and is willing to work for them some chances similar to those that rich kids with well-connected parents received at birth.

## Catching Up with the Silver Spoon

Let's say that you are an automobile mechanic dressed up for the evening in a Nik-Nik printed Banlon shirt. You meet a nice quiet girl at a disco and drive her home in your Camaro to a great big house in Lake Forest or Bedford Village or Burlingame. She invites you in. You get the impression that her parents are not delighted. You are right. Their reaction might be a shade more cordial if you could say that you were really a struggling novelist and had the vocabulary to lend your story credibility. They might warm up a little more if you could claim you were leaving in September to take up your scholarship at M.I.T. and already were tinkering in your basement with a gadget destined to make automobile batteries any bigger than a cigarette pack obsolete.

In that case, the family could hope that Mindy would forget you after you went away, or, if your gadget or book actually did boost you into the seven-digit income category, they might be willing to take you in hand socially. But if you are content with the life you have now and are just interested in meeting a nice quiet girl, look elsewhere. Your picture and Mindy's family's picture of basic survival are too different. You would not be happy with each other.

If what attracted you was simply a soft-spoken young woman who wore scarcely any makeup and smelled of something very clean, then become more alert in your own neighborhood in the daytime, join a mixed Bible study class or take a poetry course at the community college, look over your female classmates, and experiment at soap and perfume counters until you find the right present to give to some quiet girl who thinks you already make a terrific living. If you do happen to be interested in moving up socially and financially, there are circles between Mindy's house and yours where entry might be more comfortable.

If you are responsible and competent at the work you do now, you might start saving and scheming to open your own business. Sometimes you can begin to build a network in the process of looking for financial backing. New entrepreneurs don't stop at banks. They try every kind of businessman around who might be persuaded to invest in a growth venture. Even the people who don't help you the first time won't mind hearing about your progress if you are successful. Some of them could become future investors and part of your new social network. Some might have fastidious, soft-spoken daughters or sisters or cousins who would consider you a catch.

You don't have to start a business to make new contacts with affluent people, but you do have to develop some sort of interests, knowledge or skills that appeal to them. An athletic skill or a vocational skill donated a few hours a week to a civic organization supported by the well-heeled would be a possibility. Reading the newspapers and some history books, becoming informed, and joining a political or community cause that interests prosperous property owners is another.

Rich people's children develop networks through their families, schools, clubs and the locations of the homes in which they grow up. Childhood summers on the beach at Chatham on Cape Cod lead to a lot more Ivy League and power politics associations than summers on the beach at Brighton Private in Brooklyn. For others to develop networks, they must spend time in activities in which there is continuity, common purpose and opportunity for them to become known to people in the circles in which they wish to travel. (Chapter

8 discusses these in detail.) It is also important to observe the manners and tastes of these people and learn to practice them enough to makes oneself and the others comfortable. Bringing a bottle of wine, a jar of fancy mustard, or a bouquet of flowers in hand to a dinner party is a custom close to obligatory in many middle-class circles. It is seldom practiced in upper-class ones where the prompt thank you note still flourishes. Women tend to be better at picking up these details than men, but this is a matter of early training, not biology. Men can learn.

It is useful for any man or woman seeking to move up through social networks to develop skills and knowledge that make him or her a desirable personal companion. Such a companion might be a good bridge or tennis partner, an informed shopper, a willing guest or escort at the spur of the moment, or an available ear on the telephone at midnight. If you need certain people more than they need you, you often will have to be available on the schedules they choose. If you want to be included you can't be too proud or too lazy to fill in as a last minute dinner guest, even if you have to cancel your poker night or give away concert tickets.

However, you should not do anything that seriously jeopardizes your career or your educational goals. If filling in at the Van Lucre's dinner table means you have to skip the real estate broker's licensing exam you have been preparing for all year, that is too much. Unless, of course, your wedding date to the sole heir to the Van Lucre millions is firmly set. If it is, and your career plans are known to your fiancé and prospective in-laws, then you might question the situation you are getting into. Will there be any place at all for the things that matter to you in the future?

## Unequal Work, Unequal Pay

When the goal is a particular class of people, networks usually do not develop automatically. Skills in courting, other than the romantic variety, are required. The mover-up will need to become accustomed to making overtures, getting rejected, trying again. It is important to find things one really likes about these people, other than their money. Then when the mover-up expresses admiration, it rings true. Ingenuity and energy are required in finding ways to keep up and reciprocate with people who have a lot more money.

If you can't take them to La Cote Basque or the Jockey Club (where they can take you if they want to), you may have to spend some time developing convincing expertise on the cuisine of the hidden-away little ethnic restaurants where you can afford to pick up the check. If they invite you to be a house guest and you have no way of reciprocating directly, you may encourage future invitations by becoming extremely clever at finding bread-and-butter presents that precisely fit a need or a liking you have observed in your hosts. If your host mentioned his interest in a particular out-of-print book, you might track it down in the secondhand bookstores. If your hostess is fond of a set of unusual placemats, you might find an extra set of luncheon napkins that complement them perfectly. You might have your aunt send you a regional cheese or honey or variegated geranium cutting. Or you might bring back a fresh-caught fish packed in ice because that was what made your host's eyes light up at the mention of your home town. Those modest personal touches are not appreciated by everyone, but they can help a lot to endear you to some people. You'll never know which is which, or who is who, until you try.

If your rich, married woman friend with a full-time career invites you to dinner after a working day, she can breeze in from the office five minutes before you arrive. The clothes in her closet are always clean and pressed, the buttons secure. Her housekeeper has cooked dinner, set the table, walked the dog, fluffed up the sofa cushions, and is about to get out the ice for drinks. If the housekeeper is half of a couple, the service should be even smoother. When you reciprocate, if you work full-time, have no servants, and live in much smaller quarters, a little dinner for three or four or six at the same hour will take days of logistical planning, cooking ahead, living with a dining table opened and set a day or so in advance and maybe leaving the office an hour early to get things started. You can't reciprocate on a weekend, because your friends are always away, at their country house.

Richer friends can be unwittingly cruel and fickle. Someone who always has had money and the options it buys simply thinks differently from someone who hasn't. It's like the old advertising story about the agency that prepared a campaign to run on a Sunday afternoon TV program. The account executive flew to Palm Beach to present it to the client at home. The client liked the campaign but thought that a Sunday afternoon program was a poor choice. No one would hear it, because "That's when everybody is out playing polo."

The born-rich, married woman with a not-for-profit career scheduled at her convenience may get annoyed and insulted when a friend is seldom available for lunch and won't commit herself to a regular tennis night. The friend is putting in sixty or seventy hours a week developing the professional career that spells her only independent route to decent, middle-class survival. The rich woman can't imagine that anyone really has to work that hard.

If Cal Bucksborn, sole heir to a booming family business, decides on Wednesday that he really needs a long weekend to unwind at La Samanna right now, he probably can arrange it. Perhaps you've met some version of Cal, and he invites you to come along. You say you'd love to, but your presence is absolutely required at the office this Friday. You don't even mention that he hasn't exactly said he's paying. You're not sure you'd want to be that obligated to him if he had. But you'd have to save for a long time before you could blow three or four thousand dollars on a weekend trip. Cal, approaching you as a social equal, assumes that you have the same options for spending time and "small" amounts of money that he has. So he begins to think of you as some kind of grown-up grind. Your behavior is likely to be criticized as stemming from a characterological flaw rather than accepted sympathetically as economic necessity.

Listen to Cal's cousin, Martha, talking about a husband and wife team who live by their sharp and critical intellects, in journalism positions that offer more prestige than cash. Martha knows that the woman was a moving and gifted actress in college and still loves the theater. Choosing another kind of work simply because it brings a steady income is incomprehensible to Martha. She believes the real reason is simply the woman's failure of confidence in her own talent. Martha adores her friends' parties and the scintillating names she meets there. But her hosts live on a shabby street in a neighborhood scheduled for gentrification yet still a little dangerous around the edges. Martha experiences her friends' choice of location as poor taste and rudeness. She cannot grasp the idea that the higher rents of an established "nice" neighborhood really could be beyond the reach of anyone she knows.

Notice, however, that Martha's friends have something special to offer that appeals to her—their circle of scintillating celebrated intellects. So she invites them to parties despite their "lapses" from standards. Other hostesses find other attributes desirable. When Samantha was single, she was invited by hostesses who wanted to flatter and titillate a single male dinner guest. Pace Dollarson was invited because she was cheerful and patient with the pompous bores and the world-weary.

When I first began training and working as a psychotherapist, I was flattered to find myself being invited to the homes of newly met and very distinguished people in the field of psychoanalysis. I was briefly inclined to consider them kind in taking an interest in a fledgling. I quickly discovered that in certain traditional, highly competitive professional circles in New York, one of the essentials for maintaining status was to include one or two known achievers in the arts in every social gathering. In a pinch, the wife or widow of a distinguished artist would do. That status was the sole basis of most of those invitations to me. I could have been self-righteously insulted and stayed away, but those gatherings provided access to useful information and an occasional potential friend. It was a reasonable trade. Samantha's tradeoff was the opportunity to meet a great variety of eligible men in protected settings. So goes network-building in action.

## Maximum Thrust

Some network builders are more aggressive and consistent than others. Wendy was a photographer of minimal talent who set out to give herself a recognizable professional label by specializing in photographing artists. She would pursue them, offer to photograph them free at first in order to build up an impressive portfolio. When her grandmother remarried and moved to Arizona, Wendy borrowed the little duplex off Park Avenue that her grandmother was not ready to sell and passed off the apartment and its crystal chandeliers as her own. She decided to become an authority on contemporary artists. She found new ways to meet them. She might hear that the color field painter Marvin Dribblar and the action painter Chester Splashforth had never met. She would call Marvin and tell him that Chester was eager to meet him and was coming to lunch on Tuesday. If Marvin accepted, she would call Chester and tell him that Marvin hoped so much to meet him at lunch on Tuesday. If Chester accepted, Wendy met two new artists and ingratiated herself enough so that she got a chance to add them to her portfolio. She sold some of the photographs to magazines. Later, they turned up in her book, *The Contemporary I*, which she launched at a trendy gallery with a champagne party for three hundred carefully selected names.

Wendy replaced the chandeliers with the track lights appropriate to the instant treasures accumulating on her grandmother's borrowed walls. (There were some gifts and modest purchases mixed in with her own work.) In the course of expanding her network and her professional reputation, she met one of the most famous and richest of contemporary painters. He had just separated, tentatively, from his wife. Unsophisticated about the mechanics of life outside his studio, he gratefully allowed her to become his guide and arranger. They talked of marrying and even bid on an old firehouse that could be converted into his and hers studios plus living space. However, at close range, the painter's dependence on alcohol and multiple flirtations to ward off paralyzing despair diminished his appeal.

Accompanied by Wendy, of course, the painter was frequently invited to dinners given by board members before exhibition openings at major art museums. The host at one of these was a self-made financier who had become one of the museum's biggest contributors. He and his wife clearly were not getting along. Wendy sent him a copy of her book—to his office—with a charming note saying that she was considering expanding her photographic coverage to include patrons of the arts. Wendy and the financier are now ensconced—married—in a large and handsome penthouse apartment with panoramic views.

## Getting Around

People who are successful in forming networks for upward mobility and the pursuit of a worthwhile spouse are tireless about getting out, getting around, making connections and staying in touch. They are sensitive to their chosen circles' requirements in manners and customs, but they don't mind making fools of themselves once in a while for a worthy cause—their own.

The networks available to each individual vary according to idiosyncratic combinations of person, place and timing. The maintenance engineer who can coach a boys' school soccer team will develop a different network from that of the microbiologist who plays viola in an amateur chamber ensemble. Both have possibilities for upward mobility. Individuals who are active, expansive and alert to what is going on around them are in a much better position to meet an eligible spouse than those who stick to the same old haunts and the same kinds of people they always have known or limit their outings to the single-minded and often futile pursuit of that one perfect, rich, available person.

An expanded pursuit of upscale social networks requires getting used to coping with people who are not exactly mirror images of one's own ideal. Those who want to move up have to learn that a satisfactory social evening does not necessarily consist of five hours spent gazing into the eyes of Mr. or Ms. Right. Six brief, informative or amusing exchanges with four different people in the course of a cocktail party or a committee meeting can also constitute a satisfactory evening and one that demonstrates a much greater and more sophisticated variety of social skills. When the upwardly ambitious are able to find whatever is good in whatever circles they reach, they are working on making their own lives richer. They are likely to be more interesting and have more to offer when someone they'd really like to marry comes along.

In the meantime, the movers-up develop lives that encompass a worthwhile variety of people and purposes. In developing and expanding their personal networks, they are gaining access to helpful information. They are providing themselves with the protection of respected connections. They are enhancing their individual attributes with the rosier image anyone acquires through association with people and places considered glamorous or important to others.

# 6

## Signals, Stereotypes and Decoys

### A Grab Bag of Clues

*M*oney and prestige are not always obvious. They may be obscured behind regional accents, undistinguished behavior, modest tastes and ordinary, unsophisticated pursuits. Or they may be hidden deliberately. When riding through poor neighborhoods, a frightened dowager sits up front with the chauffeur, whose uniform cap has been removed. (The car is an ordinary gray sedan.) She doesn't put on her jewelry until she arrives at her destination. Many of the younger rich, in an attempt to blend in with the less favored, adopt a downgraded vocabulary. They refer to the uniformed employee waiting with the limousine as the driver and to the live-in servant who takes care of the children as the baby sitter. However, if the heir to a diversified New England banking fortune always travels coach and tourist class, this habitual thrift may be less a disguise than an ingrained form of piety.

Money and upper-class breeding may appear to be present and turn out to be an illusion. Some of the people who turn up in distinguished circles will be using the same techniques explained here in order to endow themselves with gilt by association and allow the rich to be at ease in their presence. People have been known to go to great lengths to appear well-off. Backgrounds get invented and substantiated with convincing details and the assistance of the good manners and foggy memories of supposed old cronies. Expensive cars, furs, jewels and men's evening clothes get rented—and occasionally charged to someone else's account. Women's clothing gets borrowed from designers or friends or is worn once very carefully and returned to the store with the price tag re-attached. Some people have a brief windfall or access to credit. They live high for now and keep their fingers crossed for the future.

The easiest way to find out if someone has money is to be told just how much he has by a person who is in a position to know. However, the people who may be best informed about someone's financial position often are those bound by professional confidentiality not to tell: lawyers, accountants, bankers, investment managers, psychoanalysts. Others who can talk if they want to, such as a relative who was mentioned in the will, a disgruntled former employee or business partner, an ex-spouse or an old school roommate, may not be fully informed or may make estimates that are skewed by personal bias. Nevertheless, when these people turn up in a network they can provide starter clues. While some of the ultra-rich have more money than most of us can imagine, many of the people considered rich in a given community may have far less than is supposed. Envy has a way of making moderate wealth expand in the eye of the beholder.

Many of the clues to money and privilege are subtle. Within the same financial bracket there are variations according to class, region and ethnicity. What's tacky in Bryn Mawr may be to die over in Newport Beach. A feast in Myopia Hunt country may be poverty rations in Great Neck. Casual in Oak Bluffs may be dressy in Mendocino. Esoteric in Ann

Arbor may be corny in Cambridge. In addition, there are the discordant standards of different categories of the moneyed: the Old, the New, the Snob, the Slob, the Useful and the Useless, the Statustocracy and the many varieties of middle-class prosperity.

There are clues that refer only to background and not to present social or financial condition. There are clues to future high earnings or inheritances. But there are no hard and fast rules. There are personal differences as varied as individual human beings can be. So while certain stereotypes having to do with possessions, pastimes and manners are associated with money and privilege, there are people with plenty of each who do not fit any of the stereotypes. Demonstrated confidence about the existence of options in most areas of life may be the most reliable clue to wealth of one kind or another, but there really is no single clue to money or position that is reliable. Cumulative information is required, based on frequent observation and varied exposure to the way a person lives and to the other people he or she knows. And of course different seekers of upward mobility have different goals. Many may have hidden connections in their own lives, re-trievable people from the past or overlooked people in the immediate surroundings, who could give the development of their networks a big boost.

## *Quality*

It is easier in many situations to spot a background of Old Money wealth than to figure out whether or not the person from that background has any money now. On initial acquaintance, New Money people often are indistinguishable from people who spend everything they have in the one area in which we notice them: clothing, a hobby, an expensive car, dining out. While "money" and "class," as in upper-class background, often have very little to do with each other in the present, our imaginations cling to certain stereotypes that may be outdated but are by no means extinct. They are linked to images of a life polished by the results of painstaking effort applied to excellent raw materials. Solidity, innate luster, perfection of detail are what count.

The image extends not only to things but to people carefully trained for specific roles. Along with the high-slung, big-wheeled pram go the starched English nanny, the ramrod back and taciturn deference of the English butler. We conjure twittery French governesses and ladies' maids, stern German or Scottish housekeepers, tough, athletic chauffeurs capable of grappling all day with the hard steering of a 1930s Rolls Royce and of teaching the sons of the house to play baseball as well as to drive. Moving West, we picture Oriental houseboys gliding about on silent feet and platoons of Spanish-speaking gardeners. Or South: corps of plump, smiling, soft-spoken help at the doors and in the kitchens.

We think of steep-roofed Tudor mansions bordered by masses of flowers and stately trees, of transplanted Ile de France chateaux, jaunty piles of chiseled, yellow-gray stone astride long sweeps of lawn, or of the broad, symmetrical, brick or clapboard rectangles and corniced eaves of Georgian manor houses with Palladian windows over central halls. Or we see a narrow town house with three stories of tall, shuttered windows set behind a high garden gate on a quiet street of similar gates and houses. Or mellow leather couches and oil paintings of old sea battles hung between towering mahogany shelves filled with volumes in gold-tooled bindings in the velvet-draped library of a solid row house with a somber brownstone front. Or crystal chandeliers and pale Aubusson carpets, a pair of tapestry-covered Louis Quinze fauteuils flanking a tambour table in gleaming, subtly shaded marquetry, high up in the muted pastel drawing room of an eighteen-room apartment overlooking a park.

We see thick Irish tweeds in the colors of heather, the

grainy weave and easy wrinkle of pure linen, the subtle sheen of fine, monogrammed broadcloth under thick, perfectly seamed flannel, leathers that gleam on the feet and in the hand in tones of old wine and brandy, creamy folds of silk gathered into the cuffs of blouses, handworked lace bordering crepe-de-chine slips and charmeuse bedjackets, the swirling dark patterns of rep bathrobes. We feel the smooth thickness of cashmere, the dense, soft bristle of sable, the pliant, aromatic nap of thin suede against the body, the cold weight of heavy gold links at the wrist.

We picture billowing white sails, gleaming brass fittings, teak decks manned by tanned, agile people with straight, white teeth and sunstreaked hair. We see immaculate, wide-aisled stables, horses munching quietly behind the dark boards and iron bars of big box stalls and, emerging from pine-panelled tack rooms adorned with shelves of engraved silver urns and platters and rows of satin rosette ribbons, rosy-cheeked young people in pegged breeches and high boots settled in at the ankles, carrying their hard-domed, peaked velvet caps and arguing the merits of stone wall versus post and rail fences.

We see a black Cadillac Brougham, a Jaguar XK150, a Mercedes 220SE parked in front of an Episcopal church where hatted, white-gloved ladies emerge escorted by men in narrow, subtle pinstripes. They murmur discreet greetings and promises to look into the little matter at the club or to invite a nearly grown son over for a talk about his plans. We hear light consonants and emphatic vowels emanating from a firm lower jaw and think Buckley-Andover-Yale or Brearley Farmington-Vassar. We imagine coming out parties, boxes at the opera, diplomatic receptions. We expect to hear about tense moments at the Junior Singles matches and favorite corners of the Louvre or the Prado familiar since boarding school days, along with that special little glove shop on the rue Faubourg Saint Honoré and a nice old silver dealer on Beau-

champ Place. We can see them checking in to the Georges
V, Claridge's, the Hassler, the Gritti Palace, dining yesterday
at Chez Point les Pyramides, today at Taillevent and l'Au-
berge de l'Ill.

These scenes still exist. Many of them could turn up in
the pasts of the upper-class people you meet, but even Old
Money has many variations. The heavy Georgian silver sal-
vers on the Queen Anne sideboard may contain chicken à la
king and canned peas. The members of the richest old family
in a particular countryside may drive around in a red Ford
pick-up, a twelve-year-old Volvo station wagon or a brand
new Honda Civic. They may speak in the flat, nasal vowels
or the slurred syrup tones of a particular region. They may
live in a sprawling new splanch or a converted industrial loft,
a damp and seedy Victorian pile or a low-ceilinged box of a
modern apartment. They may dress out of Sears Roebuck
and Tog Shop catalogues and eat tuna out of the can. They
may hunt with deer rifles and tend their own gardens. The
kids may go to the state university or drop in and out of
schools and work on commercial fishing boats.

Inherited old wealth offers leeway for confident eccen-
tricity. A Degas may hang forgotten in a guest bedroom. The
crack in the powder room mirror may go unrepaired for a
decade. An Aston Martin may sit in the garage for as long,
because no one is feeling sporty. The housekeeper may be a
middle-aged flower child on methadone maintenance. The
plain brown mink left hanging in the closet winter and summer may have turned ratty. But, when called upon, for funerals, board meetings, wedding receptions and occasions of
state, those raised on Old Money are almost always capable
of turning up appropriately. Their attire may not be exactly
in fashion. Undramatic in cut, favoring greys and navy blues,
with a striped school tie or a gold circle pin and one strand
of pearls, it may be a little dull but it will be absolutely correct.
In summer, at the yacht club or the golf club, they'll blossom
in lime green and raspberry pink.

They will enunciate clearly, speak in whole sentences and without grammatical error. Their manners will be perfect and effortless. They will use the right forks. They will remember family trees and property lines and which topics should be avoided. No matter how unwelcome they actually find a new guest, they will be graciously attentive and make sure that the person is always included in someone's conversation. They may notice whether a Mozart sonata is being played well or badly. They may identify the likely provenance of a newly discovered old Windsor chair. They may come up with Mother's maid's formula for removing wine stains or a telling anecdote about a current head of state who went to school with Father.

## *Labels and Luxuries*

A background of money—Old or New—may be revealed by familiarity with a range of advantages and luxuries. Spot it in someone who refers to a favorite, child-sized corner in a large, well-situated house or to traveling regularly between comfortable, seasonal homes. Notice it in references to old servants, well cared-for pets of registered breeds, early use of sophisticated athletic equipment and equipment for scientific and artistic pursuits, travel that contributed to a refined palate and historical or political awareness in childhood and adolescence. Find it in the unquestioned expectation of access to people of importance and influence, in familiar ease with a large variety of expensive articles and luxurious services, in a history of exposure to superior educational opportunities at private day and boarding schools, at Ivy League or Seven Sister colleges, or small institutions with special atmospheres, such as Sarah Lawrence and Reed. These clues to background come up in present behavior and in casual, conversational references to past experiences.

While the children of the rich are not necessarily free from anxiety and pressure to achieve, they often reveal a relaxed

assurance that they will have choices, that there will be second or third chances. They often display an ease in negotiating obstacles that someone with a less privileged history
would consider insurmountable. They are not quite so worried about missing the last train, because it occurs to them
that they could always hire a car. If the personnel officer isn't
interested, perhaps the president of the company might be.
If the library is closed, Mother's old friend, the chargé d'af-
faires, may remember the needed information, and it's not
too late to call him at home in London.

Of course, it also happens that those who grow up rich
become accustomed to having their own way and can be quite
disagreeable when thwarted. The aristocratic ideal balances
discipline and responsibility with privilege and advantage.
Superior position is supposed to be earned anew by each
generation. Aristocratic children were often brought up by
strict nurses and governesses, sent to rigorous summer camps
and to schools whose founding standards required strenuous
physical and mental effort. But the children of the newer
rich—and some of those of Old Money (standards do slip)—
have been raised in more indulgent and pampering ways.

Their rooms have been done and redone by expensive
decorators to fit their changing images or those of their parents. They have been given professional-caliber cameras,
three-hundred meter diving watches, and concert-grade musical instruments. Every advantage has been pressed on them:
ballet subscriptions, summer language residences in Oaxaca
or Aix-en-Provence, private lessons in tennis, riding, skiing,
plastic surgery to perfect noses, ears and chins. The schools
and camps favored by New Money not slavishly imitating
Old (as well as by some rebellious products of Old Money)
tend to stress attention to the needs of the individual personality and to prize most highly the individual's potential
for creative expression. Admirable in theory, in practice this
training can produce petty tyrants excessively absorbed in

their own overvalued personal whims and unable to cope with small failures, rejections or disappointments.

The grown children of New Money, like their parents, tend to be more caught up than the children of Old in surrounding themselves with material luxuries and in taking pleasure in displaying these things. New Money likes labels. New Money (in other than the Slob category) knows exactly how much less—or more—you paid for your watch or coat or shoes than it did for its own. New Money refers to its Guccis, its Pratesis, its Calvins, its Limoges, its Bang & Olafsons, its Garlands, its Hermès, its Santos, rather than to its loafers, its sheets, its slacks, its dishes, its hi-fi, its stove, its bag, its wristwatch. Old Money takes the fact of possession for granted. The stated concerns are excellence, taste, discernment, posterity. The courteous face-to-face behavior of Old Money is completely unselfconscious. The courtesy of New Money can be erratic or exaggerated.

Some of the differences between Old and New Money emerge in vocabulary. Old Money has been taught to speak grammatically from childhood and expects that everyone else can do the same. So the children of Old Money like to take expressive shortcuts among familiars. Words of one syllable, contractions and nicknames for much-frequented places, and selected crude slang are a natural part of their repertoire. Parents become "Ma" and "Pa" ("Mam*ma*" went out with the Eleanor Roosevelt generation); "flicks" for movies; "Washburg" for Washington. When I was in college in the 1950s, before four-letter words became fashionable, I noticed that it was the graduates of aristocratic New York girls' schools who most boldly appropriated the vocabularies of construction workers to punctuate their speech.

In an age-old misunderstanding of refinement, New Money tends to favor the most elaborate, indirect, multisyllabic way of saying things. New Money ladies go to luncheon. Old Money has lunch. New Money people purchase a home.

Old Money buys a house. If New Money has a summer cottage, Old Money has a place. When it has really arrived, New Money acquires an estate in the country. Old Money is more likely to have a farm, or simply a house. The house may be set in the middle of three hundred acres, with five or six outbuildings. New Money summers at the Hamptons, in the Berkshires or the Dolomites. Old Money goes to the beach or to the country. New Money has been known to extend an invitation to an affair, while Old Money asks people to dinner, has a party, or maybe gives a bash. New Money has to powder its nose or find the little girls' room. Old Money has to go to the bathroom, or something more explicit.

## Personal Checklist

Money in the past does not necessarily mean money in the present. However, it may signify privileged connections or expectations of money in the future, through inheritance or superior opportunities for employment or investment. Frequent exposure to the alleged rich person's friends, family members and other associates allows for discreet, firsthand investigation of the financial situation. When exploring the possibility of money or favored position in the present, frequent exposure is also required to sort out the truly well-to-do from those who can jump into the pool of affluence with a big splash but can't swim. Regular contact with others in the person's life is useful here, too. However, the observer should know enough about the cost of things and the standards to which different types of affluence adhere to be able to make his own informed estimates. Appearance, clothing, transportation, residences, recreation, services, and certain intangibles are natural areas for firsthand observation.

*Appearance.* When we look at a rich, privileged person, what do we see? There often is a look about those who grew up in affluence, even the middle class-variety. Whatever the genes could not provide, money to pay for orthodontists, dermatologists, orthopedic surgeons and first class haircutters could. The deeper the well-bred roots, the greater is the preference for relying on basic endowment rather than superficial cosmetic improvement. A rough rule of thumb would be: the older the money, the plainer the hairdo and the scarcer the make-up and nail polish.

Affluent upbringings usually offer good nutrition, healthy exercise and high standards for personal hygiene. The good posture that rich children are taught is both physical and mental, a stance for being at ease in the world. In practice, some girls' school graduates stride through life as if they were still on the hockey field. Some maintain the hollow-chested stoop they developed when they shot up ahead of the boys. Though they may have chosen to forget it, they were taught that ladies, in walking, allow the pelvis to move only in a front and back motion, never from side to side.

*Clothing.* On first encounter, clothing may be more a guide to personality than to money. However, a steady and ample supply of money from somewhere, particularly New Statustocracy money, comes to mind when the eye is confronted with any sizable accumulation of the kinds of items found in the upper price ranges of the Nieman-Marcus catalogue, in the boutiques of Beverly Hills' Rodeo Drive, in the average store within two blocks of New York's Fifth Avenue and Fifty-Seventh Street, or the stretches of Madison Avenue in the Sixties and Seventies. This is the territory of one hundred twenty-five thousand dollar natural Russian snow lynx belly coats, seven thousand dollar eighteen-karat gold and stainless steel wristwatches, and six hundred dollar crocodile shoes.

With Old Money, style is weighed against convenience

and ends up changing slowly, if at all. New clothes are considered not quite comfortable. There is little reason for fashions in jewelry to change when Grandmother's pearls, Mother's brooches and Father's cufflinks can be passed along to successive generations. Furs exist (though never for men), but what used to be known as the Republican plain cloth coat is still very much in evidence in the daytime. In the wide middle ground of moderate affluence, and along the road between Old Money and No Money, rigorous choices often have to be made. A substantial house or cooperative apartment, good schools for the children, travel to maintain connections, the pursuit of compelling cultural interests, often are valued more than expensive and stylish clothing.

Sometimes the really rich have been so sheltered from other people's ways of coping that they don't have the faintest idea where to find inexpensive sports clothes or bags or costume jewelry. They can be amazed at the attractive, budget-priced items in which a newcomer is turned out. However, it sometimes is difficult to tell whether they are utterly charmed and genuinely curious or whether they are smoothly vicious, putting someone on in order to put them down. This is one of the chances the upwardly mobile take.


*Transportation.* The transportation people use provides clues to money, but, like any other item, only as part of the larger picture. A Mercedes, a Porsche, a BMW, a Datsun 280ZX cost a lot, but it may be an individual's only luxury. Keeping a car garaged in an expensive city where the monthly parking fees equal the cost of another room in an apartment could indicate a broader range of access to comfortable options.

Public commuter transportation sometimes offers choices of comfort and efficiency depending on willingness to pay. If your new acquaintance commutes by rail to the office or the weekend place, does he or she travel regularly in the extra fare parlor car? Or use a reserved-seat express bus service? In some waterfront cities, a few top-level executives commute via very expensive private boat pools.

How does the person travel for pleasure? Spending their own money for first-class air fare often separates the really rich from the merely affluent. Some commute by air to weekend houses a hundred miles or so away. Some charter private planes or helicopters for the purpose and provide transportation for guests, too.

One measure of affluence is the distance and cost of travel to second and third homes, especially if they are used frequently. Trips from Phoenix to Maui, Milwaukee to Kiawah, Baltimore to St. Moritz have a way of adding up. Some two-career marriages are based in different cities and survive on regular weekend commuting. Does that sort of expense figure in your measure of affluence?

Does your new acquaintance take public transportation to and from airports? Rely on taxis? Or arrange to be met by a car? In northern cities in winter, at the theater, exhibitions, receptions and at airports with flights to the tropics, it is easy to spot the people who have chauffeur-driven cars waiting. They don't wear coats.

What about luggage? While that Boston banker may stuff his papers into a plastic, zippered case from the Harvard Coop and carry on a nylon garment bag, people who check through those sharp-cornered, leather-bound, hard suitcases that cost thousands of dollars usually are revealing a clue to their ability to afford a few other amenities. The rich don't have to worry about excess baggage charges, but, psychologically, they are better equipped to travel light. They know they can buy whatever they need along the way. Or they know it is stored in the second or third home to which they are traveling. One rich man's version of the ideal way to travel around the world was without any luggage at all. He claimed he would buy a new shirt and underwear at each stop and leave the soiled ones behind.


*Living Quarters.* Houses and apartments offer major clues about their owners and occupants, again in a context of other knowledge about the person. Some less than affluent people find that a beautiful house makes life worthwhile, and they make many sacrifices to maintain one. Some very rich people, their minds on other things, would just as soon live in a furnished hotel suite. But, in general, housing reflects an individual's financial status, education, culture, habits and priorities.

A glance at any page of real estate ads will show that property costs more when neighborhoods are considered safe and schools good, when successful people congregate there, when land is deeded or zoned in large parcels, and when there is a view. A water view if there is a body of water, a view across the valley in hilly country, a golf course or woods when the alternative is other people's houses. In big cities, height, light and a view of the sky, the park, a body of water, distant landmarks, anything but the neighbors' windows, are valued. Conversely, a whole town house with a garden, when most other people live in high-rise apartments, is a prize.

Usually large houses and apartments cost more to buy and maintain than small ones, but a small place filled with exquisitely detailed, built-in, custom workmanship and batteries of electronic devices could be the most expensive of all. It definitely would be if there was also a glass-enclosed, sixty-foot swimming pool in the back yard. Pools, tennis courts, stables and kennels indicate more money spent on care and repair. Except in certain pockets of arts-oriented society where esthetic risk and individuality are status symbols, Snob Money, like Old Money, favors antiques, restorations and "good" reproductions. When confronted with original, contemporary architecture and dramatic furniture in rich materials by name designers, it is useful to remember that these things can cost more and take more courage to buy than do antiques. Contemporary pieces seldom have the re-sale value of antiques.

A big, beautiful house or apartment with a dreary, old-fashioned kitchen may indicate that the owners never cook; they eat out or have full-time servants. However, in the last two decades, gourmet cooking has become one of the most acceptable forms of conspicuous consumption for middle-class strivers and the Statustocracy. Beautiful, efficient kitch-ens for elaborate cooking and comfortable visiting can be found in many of the homes of the affluent and competitive. Elaborate bathrooms are also fashionable among those with cash to spare, especially if the bathroom functions as part of a physical fitness plan, with professional exercise equipment, whirlpool baths and saunas or steam units.

Collections of old objects and rare objects suggest money. Original paintings, drawings and sculpture, recognized vin-tage pieces or contemporary works by known artists or those represented by serious galleries (as distinguished from those that supply paintings in styles and colors to match the sofa), suggest a certain level of culture as well as money. Small details like the constant presence of fresh flowers, imported soaps, linen guest towels that require ironing, require extra money. The more homework you do in the costs of things, from sheets and flatware and electronic garage door openers, to sound systems, sculpture and tree and lawn care, the more clues you will have to the amounts of money the owner of the place has available to spend.

Multiple homes, of course, mean duplicate and triplicate expenses. A beach house or ski house that is not rented to others for all or part of a season costs more to maintain. A second house kept open for occasional use all year costs more to maintain than one that is completely closed half the year.

A caretaker in residence costs more than a look-in house watcher.

*Recreation.* The cost of recreation varies. Skiing in Vermont if you live in Boston is a middle-income sport. Flying to Alta or Klosters or Bolivia is a high-income one. If a person has a boat, does he do the maintenance, or is a captain paid to do it? What does dockage at the marina or yacht club cost? What about yacht club membership? If the person rides horseback, does he or she rent by the hour? Own one or more horses and board them? Have a barn and pasture at home? Belong to a hunt? Van to meets or to horse shows?

Does your new acquaintance enjoy the theater? On what economic level? Buys orchestra seats regularly? Takes three or four friends at a time? Invests in Broadway plays? Is a major contributor to a regional or repertory theater? Does the person frequent expensive, private membership discos? Belong to the costliest health club in town? Belong to clubs formed around special interests, membership by invitation only? Belong to conservative, old guard social clubs, membership available primarily by heredity? The dues for the last two may be lower than those for the discos and health clubs.

*Services.* What personal services are used regularly? Custom tailors, dressmakers, hairstylists, cosmetologists? Manicurists, masseurs, exercise trainers? How many of these are paid enough to make house calls? Is there a social secretary? Are the monthly personal bills handled by an accountant? Are there accounts with stockbrokers? Investment managers? Trust officers? Is there a lawyer on retainer? At what kinds of stores are there charge accounts?

What about domestic services? If your friend is a single parent, what kind of help is paid for child care? Does someone come in—or live in—to brush, wash, press and mend clothing? Are groceries ordered by phone and delivered from stores where there are charge accounts? Is there a housekeeper who does the shopping? If your host or hostess cooks, is there someone other than a relative to serve and wash up? Are bartenders and waitresses hired for parties? Or is there a full-time staff? Are caterers used regularly, for small dinners as well as large parties?

*Entertainment.* Are there dinner parties at home? How often? For how many people? Sit-down with placecards or plate-on-the-lap buffets? What kind of food and drink are served? Chili and beer? Soft shell crabs and vintage Pouilly-Fuissé? Are there cocktail parties? What quality is the liquor? And the canapes: cheese balls? steak tartare? caviar? Is personal entertaining done in restaurants? How good—or expensive—are they? Is the person and his or her preferences well known to the maitre d' and the captains? (If yes, that suggests frequent patronage and good tips.) Are there dinner dances and benefits? One guest invited or a whole table taken?

Who are the guests? Distinguished old names? Famous achievers? Power brokers? Intellectuals? Nice, dull people? Do they all seem to know each other? Are they comfortable old acquaintances, tolerant and nostalgic? Sparklers who enjoy trying to top each other? Edgy, evasive people, always keeping an eye on what's happening somewhere else in the room? (The last group suggests slippery footing in the jungle of upward strivers.)

*Four Intangibles. Energy* is a quality often associated with money. While some of the born-rich may seem bland and limited in their enthusiasms, more of them have a vigorous stride, a firm handshake, an alert presence. The self-made rich usually sizzle with energy, a quality not to be confused automatically with charm.

*Vocabulary* offers another clue to affluence. The early education of the rich and the aristocratic instills large vocabularies, which may shrink later in life through lack of use. Aptitude testers have discovered that self-made, high-level achievers tend to acquire large vocabularies, usually through reading world-class newspapers and other sources that have nothing to do with formal schooling. Being alert, aggressive and insatiably curious probably has a lot to do with it.

Most of the people who grew up in households with *servants* deal considerately with those who tend to domestic chores in their own and others' homes. Complaints about servants are never part of their social conversation. Mistakes are taken in stride; genuine incompetents are dismissed quietly, behind the scenes, and replaced. Some of the newly arrived affluent complain about servants and services in an awkward attempt to demonstrate that they really know how things should be done or as a way of letting each other know that they now can afford the finer things of life.

If a potential spouse is banking on a *future inheritance*, it is important to know a lot about the family. How many sisters and brothers and cousins are likely to have to share the inheritance? Will it be outright? If in trusts, how restrictive will they be? Is the inheritance coming from relatively young parents or from a frail old grandparent? How likely is the legator to change his or her mind? To quarrel irrevocably with the prospective heir? To remarry or redirect interests in other ways? To lose the money?

## Spending Power

There is more to consider about present money. Recent statistics estimate that there are more than half a million millionaires in the United States. That is, five out of every two thousand individuals own net assets of more than a million dollars. However, many of those millionaires would be quick to tell you that their "fortunes" are tied up mainly in assets that do not produce income or in developing businesses whose futures are still precarious. There are millionaires on paper who feel, with some justification, that they are living hand to mouth.

As a rule, no one gets rich from straight salary or fees. Tax rates are high. Saving requires iron discipline. It is chunks of capital—invested, appreciated, manipulated profitably— that give people the leeway and the leisure to stretch in the directions that attract them.

In assessing spending power consider the differences between gross worth and net worth and between net worth and liquid assets. Liquid assets represent holdings that can be converted into cash quickly. They can be important. There are many variations on being "land poor," that is, owning a lot of valuable property that produces no income and on which you can scarcely scrounge up the cash to pay the taxes. Whether it's your own big income or a rich spouse's, how much is left to spend after taxes depends on whether it's taxed as earned or unearned income or as capital gains, whether some of it is from tax-exempt bonds, whether some of your personal expenses can be charged to business and deducted, whether you are successful in convincing the I.R.S. that the tax shelter designed to put you into a lower bracket is legitimate as a potentially profitable investment.

There are many things that someone moving up should know about taxes, estates and the law, and the facts often change from month to month. A rich person can hire excellent accountants, tax lawyers and investment advisers, but anyone can get into the habit of reading financial publications regularly. For a start, there are the business and financial pages of the daily newspaper, as well as the regional editions of *The Wall Street Journal*. The stock market prices become less of a blur and more like a horse race if you pick out a few companies in key industries to follow every day. News articles about the forming, merging and dissolving of companies, about government regulations, about new product developments and the movements of executives can help you to become familiar with the language and workings of money. These studies can be pursued further in specialized periodicals ranging from the professional to the general popular level. Among the major ones are *Barron's*, *Dun's Review*, *Business Week*, *Fortune*, *Forbes* and *Money*.

Anyone staking a financial future on a marriage needs some legal advice. It is essential to learn where the law protects you and where it doesn't. If you sign a prenuptial agreement, is it legal? Do you live in a community property state, where each spouse is entitled to half the couple's total assets? If not, how much of a husband's estate must legally go to the wife? And how much of a wife's to the husband?

In one recent case, an eighty-year-old multimillionaire died after a loving and happy twenty-year marriage to a devoted woman twenty years younger than he. He left five million dollars to a nonprofit institution with which he was closely affiliated. He left bequests to his estranged children from previous marriages. He left his wife one of the three elaborate residences they had occupied and the income from a trust fund of slightly less than a million dollars. The principal could not be invaded for any reason. The income would not cover the cost of running the house. His widow knew why he had provided for her so meagerly. He considered her young and attractive enough at sixty to marry again, and he couldn't bear to think of another man spending his money. His will, and the prenuptial agreement that allowed these terms, were legal.

There are other dangers to consider if someone is banking on an inheritance from a spouse's parents. Inheritances can be doled out in dozens of different forms of trusts, only some of which give the beneficiaries access to the principal. Impossible conditions can be imposed directing many aspects of the legatee's life, which could make *married* life miserable. It is still possible to be disinherited for marrying against parental wishes. An heir or heiress might have to wait until his or her forties or fifties or sixties to receive the inheritance. Or he or she might be the victim of a favorite device of punitive and controlling parents. They pass over their own grown children on any number of pretexts, which they mention in the will so that it cannot be contested, and leave the entire estate in trust to the grandchildren, who cannot begin to collect until they are twenty-one, or thirty, or any age the legator chooses.

Even if the bride or groom is in possession of a fortune at the time of the marriage, there is no guarantee that the spouse will be able to spend it as he or she wishes or even have a say in the way it is spent. There are women in diamonds and lynx, charging the day's exercise class, pedicure and *cuisine minceur* lunch to their husbands' acounts, who don't have access to two hundred dollars in cash. There are men receiving their guests at exclusive old clubs, dressed in custom tailored suits brushed and laid out by private servants, who couldn't write a check to pay for a new set of tires for their wife's Mercedes. But their wives can.

Sometimes a rich spouse most decidedly does not want the poorer one's standard of living to rise through marriage. The heir to a greatly diminished fortune, or the self-made man already paying two alimonies, may be delighted with his middle-class wife's habitual economies. She considers him extremely generous for gifts and allowances that a woman from a wealthy background would criticize as stingy.

## The Resource File

Among the things the upwardly mobile can do to orient themselves in the worlds of the more privileged is to make field trips of many kinds. The purpose of a field trip is *study*.

The student observes people's looks and manners, picks up bits of their conversation. The observer can attend fashionable funerals and memorial services, visit the campuses—particularly the art galleries, libraries and coffee shops—of Ivy League colleges. Field trips can extend to dog and horse shows, where people stroll about informally and talk to almost anyone attending. Time can be spent on the dock where private sport fishing boats and cabin cruisers tie up. Study can include browsing in luxury stores to learn prices and become sensitive to quality.

The zealous researcher can arrange to be shown some luxury houses and apartments or pay to go on house tours, sponsored in most communities in the name of one worthy cause or another. The researcher might sit in the lobby of an expensive residential hotel, observe the people passing by, and try to distinguish the privileged from the run-of-the-mill. Further study may lead to attending openings at art galleries where the rich patrons buy, at auctions of fine antiques and valuable art works, at antique car shows, flower shows, groundbreaking ceremonies, dedications, anything run and patronized by the kinds of people selected for study. The researcher who can afford it can buy the most reasonable seats at the benefit performances society people attend, mingle in the lobby during intermission, observe details, and distinguish the hallmarks of affluence and belonging.

Only rarely will these activities result in meeting someone and continuing an acquaintance. Their purpose is to orient, to develop perception and judgment, to become comfortable and knowledgeable about the social and financial positions of the people encountered in the course of long-term network building pursuits. After your network has been expanding for awhile, however, you may run into well-connected people you know when you are out doing your field work.

Certain sections of newspapers are excellent for picking up names and details the network builder needs to know. A dedicated student gets in the habit of reading wedding and engagement announcements and obituaries. Not all newspapers are as thorough as *The New York Times* in tracing genealogies of achievement back three and four generations, but all will give some information about who is related to whom and where the social receptions and religious observances of the locally affluent and prominent take place.

A good engagement announcement or wedding announcement tells which grandfather founded what company, mentions parents' careers, lists whom they remarried if they are divorced, and names the towns where everybody lives. It lists the schools the marrying couple attended and the work they do. It mentions former marriages of the bride or groom, as well as the number of children they have, but it doesn't name the ex-spouses.

A good obituary gives a whole socioeconomic profile. It lists the deceased's lineage, if the family is historically important or socially prominent, highlights his career, names the corporate and nonprofit boards on which he served and those he chaired, states his political affiliations and club memberships, gives the locations of all his residences, mentions the existence of an extensive art collection or any other noteworthy possession in his present or past. It names present and past spouses, children, and, occasionally, names other surviving family members and tells where they live. A lot of connections can be outlined in the text of one obituary.

When paid directors or volunteer chairpersons of major cultural institutions and philanthropies are appointed, or when they leave, newspaper articles sometimes have a great deal of information about the person and his or her connections. The information is similar to that offered in sections marking more personal transitions. It is sometimes more detailed in the areas of interest to a reader seeking new connections and fields of operation. Feature articles on personalities in the business sections can give similar information. The sports pages sometimes carry articles about the owners of professional teams and racing stables. These people usually are rich. The profiles on prominent hostesses and achievers on what used to be called the women's pages can also offer useful background information.

There is a lot to keep in mind about the looks, the sounds, the behaviors of those with money and important connections. Correct reading of the clues to wealth and position evolves from the background information the seeker stockpiles for himself or herself. Some determined climbers keep cross-indexed Rolodex files on people and places. Others operate with a more general set of associations on tap in their excellent memories. As we will see in Chapter 7, a person's occupation can be examined as a clue to making money or to having it already. An individual's or a family's relationship to philanthropic, cultural and political organizations can signal money. The avocational and community interests that traditionally attract the rich—explored in Chapter 8—offer starting points for investigation. Orienting oneself to the goods and services available to the rich—and to their prices—allows the mover up to recognize the clues when he or she sees them. In becoming sensitive to signs of privilege, as in learning any new subject, skill and accuracy improve with frequent practice.

# 7

## Working Up

### Different Aims, Different Drives

*I*n America, the world of work offers the most abundant variety of options to the upwardly mobile. There is work associated with wealth and status, work in which to achieve these things, work in which to meet those who have them, and work favored by those who don't need any more of them.

People are not born with equal gifts or equal opportunities. Individuals vary in their natural endowment and aptitudes. Some environments are bleak and crushing, while others offer every advantage. Yet some people fritter away their advantages, while others find ways to grow and prosper against staggering odds. Amazing things are possible when an individual decides that something he wants is within his reach, and he is willing to do whatever is necessary to attain it. A purpose larger than the individual's own satisfaction, such as responsibility or love for others, or a moral conviction or religious fervor, often helps to focus productive energy dramatically.

Many of the people who start with little and do well tend to be those who remain flexible and who adapt, from within their range of abilities, to the opportunities they spot within their geographic and cultural communities.

Before she met Dan, the self-made multimillionaire, Hilda was married to a middle-class dreamer whose mind was seldom on his job long enough to keep it very long. Hilda would have liked to use her extra energy to go to college and become a teacher of English literature, but she realized that she would have to provide substantially for her two small children. She saw a need in her suburban town for a flexible catering service, so she pitched in and developed a successful one. It also helped her to meet Dan, when he hired her to cater a large party.

## The Bounds of Ambition

In all upward striving, there are realistic and moral boundaries. For the striver with a conscience, *what serves my needs* and *what's good for others* are frequently opposing tugs, and the balance between them is not fixed. As a rule of thumb, the greater his public contribution, the more the world is likely to excuse someone for ruthless business practices or for making a mess of his private life. However, this kind of tolerance is not always shown by those in that private life. Children, mistresses and spouses, among others, have been known to vent their rage and resentment in print. Witness such books as Christina Crawford's *Mommy Dearest*, Gary Crosby's *Going My Own Way*, Françoise Gilot's *Life With Picasso*, and Caitlin (Mrs. Dylan) Thomas' *Leftover Life to Kill*.

The realistic boundaries are seldom fixed either. Apart from the extensive and expensive training required, specific vocal equipment and a musical ear are essential for becoming an opera singer. A person in a wheelchair will probably use his time more efficiently if his work allows him to stay in one office all day rather than cover half a dozen scattered locations. Yet a young man with lower than average math apti-

tudes can be trained for highly technical work and go on for
an engineering degree in an evening program, if he really
wants that career and can accept the need for tutoring and a
lot of extra study. A woman who starts as a bookkeeping
trainee after high school can arrange to go to college part-
time and get the accounting and M.B.A. degrees that make
her eligible for high-level corporate office. People over thirty-
five have been known to go to medical school and graduate.
People who worked as domestic servants have gotten Ph.D.'s
and become heads of college departments. Successful new
careers have been started after age forty, fifty or sixty. Very
determined people arrange these things while coping with
family problems, physical and emotional difficulties, precarious financial arrangements and the care of children.

## Marriage as Work or Marriage Via Work

The hard work involved in the choice to move up to a
higher income or higher status occupation may be no harder
than the work required to find and keep a rich or an important
spouse, especially for someone who becomes dependent on
that spouse's financial support. The daily lives of Ames, Hilda
and Pace were arranged entirely around their husbands'
priorities and well-being.

In the course of succeeding at a money-making occupation, the mover-up may not have a lot of free time but may
instead gain natural access to other successful and affluent
people. He or she enters their circles as "somebody" and can
afford to keep up with them in social activities. It would not
seem strange to anyone if such a successful person were to
marry within that affluent circle. This is the major route
through which men traditionally have made successful marriages up the social and financial ladder. The wife's money
enhances the husband's other achievements but is not the
sole source of his worldly success. The wife has a husband

she and the members of her set can respect. There is reciprocity here.

Although the same kind of marital move up is also available to women, until recently, only a small proportion of the women who worked developed the kinds of business and professional careers that gave them the same socioeconomic leverage. The somewhat bigger leap up through a fortunately placed supporting role was the more traditional, though not so heavily traveled, route for women: the secretary who married the boss, the nurse who married the doctor, the student who married the professor.

There always has been a handful of career-oriented women whose marriages within their own fields helped to boost their career options and their earnings. The opportunities came from expanded social contacts within the professional circle or from direct business opportunities provided by the husband. Unless some rare expertise is required, people feel more comfortable hiring and doing business with people they know. A young actress who marries an established theatrical producer or playwright may find that she has become less anonymous. Directors remember to consider her for new roles. The insurance clerk who marries the boss and stays on in the business may become its president. The clinical social worker who marries a psychiatrist may develop a private practice out of the overflow from her husband's case load and the referral sources met through his professional affiliations. These marriages may be made deliberately for the sake of advancing a career, but they often are the natural outcome of being out in the world and engaged in something productive.

## Tracking Down Income

For the person seeking to marry up financially and considering other people's work as a guide to their earnings, it is important to remember that there are wide variations within a given field and from desk to identical desk within the same office. Salaries and fees are based on complexity of skills, amount of responsibility assumed, length of training before employment, on-the-job experience, and what the traffic will bear. Pay is driven upward when a particular kind of expertise is scarce or when there is competition for a certain individual's services.

If the person works for the government or below top management levels in a bureaucratized private company, estimates of his or her salary are not difficult to obtain. Pay is tied to identifiable factors such as job classification, title and length of service. In civil service or other government jobs, salaries are a matter of public record. So are union pay scales. Credit checks on holders of stock in public corporations and other types of property are available through lawyers and brokers. In private companies, knowledge of remuneration also comes from informed hearsay, reports by individuals who have been offered particular jobs, the ranges of salaries listed in the classified ads, a sharp eye for newspaper articles that outline an organization's progress and problems, trace the development of certain careers, and give specific figures on salaries and bonuses.

Thorough reading of the best newspaper covering a particular region will provide clues to its money-makers. They will turn up in the business, social, cultural and sports pages, as well as in general reporting of community events. The same news weeklies and financial magazines that list the richest people in the country also, periodically, publish the range of earnings associated with particular occupations or the earnings of specific individuals in different fields. The latter lists serve as rough guides to comparable occupations. Trade journals tend to be circumspect but offer some guidelines to earnings.

While the average company president earns less than a hundred thousand dollars a year, the annual salaries, bonuses and benefits of some chief executives reach close to and above two million dollars. Hierarchical nomenclature varies from place to place, but titles such as President, Chairman, Creative Director, Senior Vice President, Partner, and anything followed by "in-chief" indicate the upper reaches of whatever pay scale is operating. Farther down the line, at the middle management level, big titles are sometimes substitutes for big pay.

## Owning Versus Earning Versus Subsidized Time

Whether the aspiring mover-up chooses a line of work as a means of gaining money and prestige or uses the occupations of others as a guide to opportunities for marrying up, there is an axiom about work and money that every ambitious person should keep in mind. *It is not the money you work for, but the money that works for you that makes the difference.* Money that works whether you do or not offers the broadest options, no matter how high the earnings from your own work.

Money works through various kinds of property if the property produces income from interest, dividends or leases, or if it brings more than its purchase price and expenses when it is resold. Money also works for a person when his position supplies a steady income, fringe benefits and all the conveniences of an office but allows the holder to spend a considerable part of his time away from the office engaged in activities that are not part of the job.

These job-subsidized activities can range from personal indulgences to public-spirited causes. They might include midweek golf games, horse show judging, rendezvous with a lover or beating the weekend traffic. They might consist of chairing the hospital fund-raising drive or a campaign to beautify neighborhood streets, serving on a government investigative commission or the board of a trade association. In jobs in which there is no strict accounting for time in and

out of the office, how the individual takes care of his responsibilities is up to him. The connections made through
some of his extracurricular activities may even enhance his
value to the organization. In fact, in certain old firms, there
is often one partner whose main function appears to be to
serve on various philanthropic boards and civic committees.
The importance of extracurricular links to a broad power network in the community has long been taken for granted in
big business, banking and law.

Jobs with considerable leeway in the use of time can exist
in the highest executive and profit-sharing levels in business
and industry or in certain lower-paying but prestigious occupations. A lawyer may maintain his partnership in a fine
old firm while he takes on high-level responsibilities in a
client's corporation. A tenured professor at a private college
may carry a light teaching load and write novels or poems
or help a congressman draft legislation. Or, if he is sufficiently
reckless, he may indulge in shadier enterprises. Recently, a
high-living professor at New York University was tried and
sentenced to jail for allowing his laboratory to be used for
the manufacture and sale of drugs.

Money works, too, for the descendants of the nineteenth
century robber barons and of less flamboyant, more modern
entrepreneurs. Multiple branches of families still are supported handsomely on fortunes amassed originally from such
sources as land, natural resources, transportation equipment
and services, heavy industrial products, utilities, chemicals
and pharmaceuticals, cosmetics, clothing manufacture, publishing, the media, advertising, retail merchandising, and the
processing and packaging of foods. The very rich, having
diversified investments, may not know where most of their
money is actually coming from. But in places such as Palm
Beach, where the aging rich from all over congregate for the
winter season, people are identified less by their names than
by the original sources of their fortunes. *She's the cereal com-*

*pany. They're Fifty-Seven Varieties. He's Standard Oil of New Jersey. There go the Band-Aid people.*

## Traditional Wealth

While great fortunes differ in origin, most of them are perpetuated through a labyrinth of investments whose management requires sophisticated skills. These include banking, brokerage, accounting, tax law and fluency in regional, national and international regulations, analysis of natural resources, production, marketing, and economic and political trends. The wealthy, the children of the wealthy, and the would-be wealthy often work directly at investing, lending, insuring and managing their own money and that of other people. Someone who calls himself a banker, a stockbroker, an investment adviser or investment manager may be simply a salaried, middle-class, middle-management employee. Or he may be the possessor of a considerable fortune with aristocratic roots—or scandalous ones. Further research on that person will be required to determine his financial worth and social standing.

Investors can also lose money, of course. But loss is relative. An eight hundred thousand dollar loss from a twelve million dollar fortune probably won't affect the way the family lives for some time (in a corporation, it would cause panic among the stockholders). But a seventy-five thousand dollar loss from a two hundred thousand dollar personal nest egg could be immediately devastating. It is useful to remember that not everyone who invests or manages money does it well.

Tidy fortunes frequently are accumulated quietly by individual owners of small businesses selling high-priced luxury items or low-priced, high-volume essentials for household or industrial use. Plastic valves, electrical switches, and coordinated closet ensembles have furnished as many mansions for their producers as have fabulous jewelry and sumptuous automobiles.

The very top executives in major industries usually have six and seven digit salaries and bonuses augmented by entry into ownership through stock options and other arrangements. Partners in the mouthful-of-names law firms that specialize in representing big business and large private fortunes also tend to have incomes well up in the six figure brackets. A few lawyers in specialties such as litigation and matrimonial cases earn sums like telephone numbers, but the rule of thumb in law, as in other professions, is that the greater the amount of time spent attending to the individual human being, the lesser the income.

## *Respectable Employment*

Marrying up does not always mean marrying money or privilege, of course. Sometimes it is a matter of attaining a respectable position within a particular community. Sometimes a spouse with a decent, dependable income takes precedence over one with a distinguished degree or job title. Certain professions confer prestige on the basis of implied knowledge, disciplined training and the potential for steady employment. Most law practices are in this category rather than that of the high fliers just discussed. Doctors usually earn a good living—the national average is about seventy-five thousand dollars a year—but spectacular medical earnings are reserved for the specialties in which high fees are charged for specific procedures. Surgery heads this list, with plastic surgery at the very top. But surgeons' expenses are high, primarily for malpractice insurance, and their work schedules can be gruelling. Some other medical specialties, such as radiology and dermatology, are less subject to emergency calls. The time factor should be weighed against the top dollar in considering the quality of life with a physician spouse or with any spouse whose work demands top priority.

There is a lot of middle-class prestige attached to any sort of professional or advanced degree. Dentistry, podiatry and accounting, degrees in pharmacy, engineering, psychology, and Ph.D.s in all the sciences and humanities count. Although individual practitioners sometimes have an entrepeneurial bent and find ways to attract affluent clients and achieve big incomes, none of these professions is linked automatically to high earnings.

A skilled trade may offer more opportunity for financial gain than a college degree. A master carpenter/mechanic or a licensed plumber or electrician who starts his own small contracting business is likely to do better financially than a research chemist or an architect working in somebody else's firm. Ownership of rental buildings, such as small, multifamily dwellings and stores, that the owner can maintain himself, also has provided opportunities for accumulating capital. Immigrant neighborhoods used to be divided between those who scrimped and saved to send their children to college and those who scrimped and saved to buy buildings. The grandchildren of the successes from each group have grown up with interchangeable advantages.

## Roller Coasters and Personal Risks

No one who makes money can guarantee that he or she will keep it, but some forms of high earnings are especially precarious. Talent, for example, can be a route to success, but marriage to an undiscovered talent promises nothing but a struggle to survive. Marriage to a well-known artist or performer could offer a financial roller-coaster ride between prosperity and hard times. A very few living artists' paintings and sculptures bring six-digit sums. A handful of star performers command high fees, royalties from recordings, shares of box office earnings and other lucrative arrangements that add up to more than a million dollars a year. But most artists, writers, actors, dancers and musicians who become successful have more fame than money. The fame can function socially as a money equivalent. However, many of these people shape their lives entirely around their work. When they marry, they require dedicated and self-effacing spouses.

High earnings are also precarious in enterprises that are sensitive to small shifts in the economy. Builders, as well as providers of luxury goods and services, are in this position, though, in good times, some of them make fortunes. There are big risks, and occasional big profits, in such ventures as wildcat oil drilling, speculative real estate development, and retail franchises.

Brand new fortunes from exciting new ventures are in the roller coaster category until they have been around long enough to demonstrate stability. These are often the millionaires on paper, living on a shoestring. But some down-to-earth products, and some esoteric ones, eventually have produced spendable fortunes for their developers. Among these are hang gliders, retread sneaker soles, pet foods, frozen pizza, herbal teas, discount clothing, express package delivery, self-improvement organizations, and computer software and services. The determined marrier-up should never dismiss casually some newly met character who has a wild but persistent idea. It is prudent to arrange for further observation. The grease monkey who says he's going to own a chain of gas stations with a hundred employees may turn out to be telling the truth.

The personalities of maverick entrepreneurs tend to be as difficult as those of artists. Many are loners, willing to make big sacrifices in order to be their own bosses. They are often driven people, willing to work eighteen hours a day for many years. However, two entrepreneurial types with complementary skills can sometimes form a good partnership that includes marriage *and* a joint business venture. Trendy restaurants, flourishing tourist resorts, and high volume fashion houses have been known to emerge from this kind of energetic partnership. Sometimes the marriage evaporates but the business relationship endures.

Even riskier than the legitimate roller coasters are the unsavory and illegal money-makers: wholesale street drug dealers, organizers of rings for fencing hot goods, professional gamblers, pimps, shifty promoters and mob executives. These types have substantial sums of money passing through their hands at times and have a reputation for spending lavishly on their own pleasure and that of their consorts. Some of them operate at sophisticated, even elegant, levels out of fashionable addresses. (The professor convicted for illegal drug manufacture was distinguished in his field.) However, they obviously do not offer security or respectability, even though some of them hobnob with restless aristocrats and the Statustocracy. They do reflect doubt about the self-esteem of those who knowingly choose to take up with them.

## The Working Rich

In compiling an occupational guide to the affluent and privileged, there is another category of work to consider. This consists of vocational activities that are attractive to people who already have money and for whom a fee, salary or commission is merely a pleasant supplement to an existing income.

The arts and the fringes of the arts attract many of the independently wealthy. Painters, writers, sculptors, actors and musicians with independent incomes may live in conditions as shabby as those of their unsubsidized counterparts. But this kind of life has the thrill of a game for them. They know that clean sheets, new cars and regular meals are available elsewhere, if they want them. If an artist's or writer's work doesn't sell, if a performer seldom plays in public, if these people don't work at other paying jobs, they have incomes from somewhere, even if the income turns out to be only a social security pension for psychiatric disability.

Some cultured rich people find satisfaction in developing specialized expertise and working as museum curators. Some own offbeat art galleries, become independent film makers, run experimental theaters, start little magazines. A person who takes occasional odd jobs, such as ferrying pleasure boats from one resort to another, or who changes occupations frequently and easily, without any change in comfortable living arrangements, usually has independent income. The same is true for the developers of odd, attractive little shops, resorts and restaurants where idiosyncratic standards of quality and taste are more important than the balance sheet. These businesses often serve as tax shelters. Sometimes these activities do catch on and become profitable. Even if profit was the goal, the entrepreneur with independent means can afford to gamble longer on riskier enterprises than the one operating on nothing but a small, borrowed stake.

Another respectable activity for the children of the rich is teaching in private schools, where high intellectual standards and low student-teacher ratios are maintained, while teachers' salaries remain small stipends. Junior editorial jobs on the fashion and shelter magazines are also favorite occupations of upper-class women. Young editors at the Condé Nast publications (*Vogue*, *House & Garden*, *Glamour*) used to refer to their paychecks as their allowances. The big money-making jobs at these publications usually are on the unglamorous, business ends.

Responsibility to others is taught in the families of the Useful Money rich, and some of the children take it very seriously. Doctors and lawyers who live well but confine their practices to low-salaried, public service work either are doing something illegal on the side or have independent incomes. Politics regularly attracts those for whom money alone does not provide sufficient power.

A minor trend that emerged in the seventies was that of

the blue collar occupation for the offspring of several generations of higher-than-white-collar affluence. In certain communities in which handcrafts, natural foods and fabrics, and
personal involvement in the arts are valued (particularly
flourishing south of Fourteenth Street in Manhattan, north
of Bennington in Vermont, and west of the Sierra Nevada),
a high proportion of the carpenters, house painters, electri-
cians and plumbers turn out to be Ivy League college alumni.

## Rubbing Elbows

It is one thing to identify occupations that indicate social
standing and financial comfort. It is another to arrange to
meet the people engaged in them. The world of work offers
several paths for access. One is to go to work for a big achiever.
Occasionally the consequences are spectacular. Leona was a
star real estate saleswoman who impressed the boss in a
number of ways that led him to make her both Mrs. Harry
Helmsley and a power in a business with colossal impact on
the urban environment.

Our own Samantha, the sparkler who settled into geriatric
social work after her marriage, met her husband, Greg, when
she took a temporary job on a marketing research project for
a company he subsequently sold. Samantha was a charmer,
noticed wherever she went. She would have done well socially no matter what her job. Access to top achievers from
low level positions usually requires extraordinary personality
or ingenuity or sex appeal, combined with nerve and luck.
However, many different kinds of work offer some possibilities for contact with fortune's favorites in any community.
A person determined to marry up might choose an occupation
for its network building potential, rather than for the main
chance.

Some of the "contact" occupations are low-paid and vir-
tually invisible. Routine personal services—the work of

chauffeurs, cooks, maids, butlers, nannies, gardeners, building superintendents, doormen, waiters—merely offer exposure and an opportunity to observe the quirks and customs
of the privileged at first hand. Naturally, there are always
exceptions. A few of today's wealthy matrons, dowagers and
divorcees were hatcheck girls in the 1940s. But in spite of
them—and the *au pair* girl and the riding instructor who
marry the heir and heiress and have divorces that make head-
lines—the invisible service occupations do not offer many
sound opportunities for mingling socially with the well-heeled
and the well-connected.

However, other "contact" occupations are entrepreneurial and have somewhat more fluid social standing. Along
with exposure, they also present opportunities for someone
who is clever and ambitious to make quite a bit of money.
Hilda and Dan met when he called her catering service. He
was new in town, and his mansion was not adequately staffed
for the housewarming party he was planning. Hilda was out-
standingly helpful. Marriage does not always result directly,
but the network-building potential in these contact occupations can be vast. Interior design, catering, dress design, floral
display, landscape design, hairdressing, pet grooming, sports
instruction, the arrangements made by travel agents, all can
become star services in the right hands. And "stars" are wel-
comed socially.

Not all real estate brokers marry the boss or become the
boss, but those who sell luxury housing are bound to meet
rich people. Choosing a place to live can be an anxiety-pro-
voking process for anyone. A realtor who is sensitive to the
needs of the client, and is helpful in providing extra information and smoothing out difficulties, could become a memorable person. Strategically timed follow-up calls, to check
on how certain arrangements have functioned or simply to
inquire how the match between home and buyer is working,
may lead to a social relationship, usually one more useful in

developing the network than in making a direct catch. A currently successful New York real estate woman turns up in newspaper columns with methodical regularity as the hostess at dinner parties featuring a zesty mixture of celebrated movers and shakers, hardy Statustocrats, livelier Old Money, and the most respectable of the journalists who report on such "private" events. The hostess claims that she lives for her business and her friends and has no wish to marry, and this may be so, but she is certainly in a position to meet interesting and important men and to know when they are available.

Interior decorators and designers spend a lot of time in clients' homes. They become familiar with many intimate details of the clients' lives. They still may be dealt with across the same polite, anonymous gulf that separates master and servant, but there is often a chance that a charming designer who speaks and dresses properly may be seen as a social "find" and become a regular on the guest list or be offered such amenities as the use of the house in Acapulco. This is particularly true when the clients represent nervous New Money that would welcome a guide with taste or the lonely and empty Useless Money rich who need as many "friends" as they can get. An Old Money client seeking diversion or expert information in a previously unexplored area may opt to take up with the designer or anyone who strikes his or her fancy, for a while.

Other kinds of serious and respectable work can put people in touch with money, power and privilege, depending on location and emphasis. Journalists and photojournalists can make many opportunities for themselves. As Wendy, our photographer and multiple choice climber demonstrated so well, portrait sittings or interviews in depth sometimes open doors to continuing association. Doctors, dentists, veterinarians, private duty nurses, accountants and architects all have the potential for these kinds of productive encounters. Location and reputation play a part in realizing that potential. The editors of fashion magazines and home design or shelter magazines meet the visibly affluent while doing feature articles on their dwelling places and getting them to pose wearing the newly decreed trends. Dog breeders, horse trainers, art dealers, custom dress designers and chic boutique owners sell directly to the rich. Professional fund raisers and foundation executives also deal with rich people in the course of their work. Politicians of all persuasions need backers with money and spend time courting them professionally. Friendships often follow.

## High Visibility

Orchestra conductors, solo instrumentalists, opera stars, prima ballerinas, famous playwrights and best-selling authors are sought after socially by the culturally-minded rich. In other affluent circles, star professional athletes are prized. Fashion models often attract rich men, many of whom do not have marriage in mind and do have rather kinky preferences in intimate encounters. Models often have nothing but fashion and appearance on their minds, and the people available for a well-rounded social life find them disappointingly boring. Advertising and high fashion pay its stars several hundred dollars to pose, and some hard-working photographic models earn fortunes that they invest in second, longer-lasting careers. However, "model" is also a term that is used loosely and can turn out to be a thin cover for a call girl. Since acting has acquired middle-class respectability, with degrees in it being granted at prestigious universities, "model" has picked up the association with loose morals and prostitution that was assigned to "actress" in earlier times.

The advantage in mobility held by people whose work requires them to appear in public is that they are, literally, visible. Actors, broadcasters, musical performers, sports figures and politicians are seen and recognized by thousands of people. Public figure status is a money equivalent. It frequently gives entree to the affluent and well-connected. Even a person who was in the public eye because of a scandal becomes a bit more of a "somebody" than a well-behaved person no one has ever heard of. However, I do not advocate that anyone go out and create a scandal in order to become a public figure. Sooner or later the unpleasant consequences will outweigh the social opportunities.

Careers that lead to high visibility, or that depend on it, offer big rewards for a very few and repeated frustration and disappointment for many who choose them. Someone who cares passionately about a particular kind of work may find it worth all the risks. Someone who is only gambling on high visibility as a way of moving up socially and financially may not. One coal miner's daughter may have become a country music star. For many another, getting herself into an environment in which she could meet and marry a computer maintenance technician would be a most satisfactory step up in the world.

## Working Changes

There is still another way to use the workplace as foundation for a social network that is conducive to marrying up. It is sometimes necessary to change the nature or location of one's own work in order to get in touch with a more affluent and accessible group of people. Often, in order to become visible in a workplace where some people are high earners, the socially ambitious have to upgrade their own careers.

A topnotch secretary in a law office may be indispensable to that office's functioning, but she may date the mailroom manager or a stationery salesman or a statistics clerk. If she were able to invest ten years or more in the discipline and sacrifice required to go to college and law school at night, she could then join a firm as a lawyer and become socially visible to other lawyers. She would also have a career that allowed her to be less dependent on money coming from a marriage. Regular reading of the engagement announcements in urban newspapers reveals that, more and more frequently, men and women working in the same occupation and at the same professional level marry each other. Lawyers marry lawyers. Medical students marry medical students. (The son of a middle-class social worker married the daughter of a Rockefeller when both were young physicians completing residencies in psychiatry.) Editors marry editors. Astronauts marry astronauts.

A clerk in a real estate office may know a lot about the business and be very helpful to the sales staff and brokers. If the clerk does extra work, demonstrates eligibility for sponsorship, takes the exams and becomes a licensed broker, he or she gets out into the world of clients. Out there, as we have seen, potential high commissions and occasional interesting additions to the social network expand life's possibilities. The young man who works at a technician's job while going to college at night for an engineering degree may choose to postpone marrying until he becomes a front-office professional and is able to meet a different class of women. Or he might choose to marry early but pick a wife who shares his own long-term goals for upward mobility and is willing to do her share in working toward them.

Sometimes a change of focus within the same occupation is required for increased upward mobility. A photographer concentrating on art, making moody shots of cracks in the sidewalk and close-ups of flower petals, may make a statement that enhances other people's perceptions. Eventually, affluent admirers may be attracted to that work. But if the goal is financial and social upward mobility, the photographer would do better to snap important people at their best at public receptions and, like Wendy, seek opportunities to make portraits of achievers. Offering people something that appeals to their vanity, and that they can use in promoting themselves, usually widens one's circle faster.

Sometimes what's needed is a change in location. An individual may start as a file clerk and work up to administrator of a department in a public hospital. In that setting, the administrator deals with bureaucracy, a changing staff of newly immigrated foreign professionals, and a patient population composed almost entirely of the poor. That administrator could take the same work skills to a prestigious, voluntary, teaching hospital. There, a similar job offers contacts with doctors and patients who make money and who sometimes come from wealthy and prominent families. Contacts with rich volunteers and board members could also be within the realm of possibility.

An attractive, personable man teaching at a big city college might find the marriage prospects more socioeconomically appealing if he managed to find a job, even at a cut in salary, at a prestigious, expensive, private women's college. To land that job he might have to exert himself first to get some papers published and establish a reputation in his field. In any teaching position, some of his students are bound to fall in love with him each semester. At the private college, there is greater likelihood that some of these smitten scholars would be from prominent families. Realistically, a woman professor's options are not the same. The prevailing preference in our society remains the older man–younger woman combination. The woman professor might have discreet affairs with her male students, but she would risk loss of respect from colleagues if she married one. The male professor's image would not be damaged by his marriage.

Not all career switches reflect an attempt to move up or marry up. (My own decision, in the late 1960s, to get a graduate degree in social work and train to work as a psychotherapist at the bottom of the mental health hierarchy represented a lowering of social and financial sights according to the values of the high-income, publicly influential circles in which I moved in those days.) Sometimes, for those not born rich and well-connected, a career decision to focus on matters of importance to oneself at the sacrifice of opportunities for upward mobility is comfortable only after a certain amount of proving oneself has taken place. Recognition at work or satisfaction in personal relationships, savings accumulated or self-awareness and confidence gained, all can be forms of proving oneself.

## Good Prospects and Hard Times

Opportunities for meeting prospective marriage partners, or for forming an upwardly mobile network that leads to suitable marriage partners, should not be confused with sex at the office. Sex at the office may look too easy and enjoyable to pass up, but it can result in sticky complications, enduring resentments and, when things become too uncomfortable, the resignation or firing of one of the participants.

The most appropriate social use of the workplace is for building up those extended networks through which a desirable mate emerges. When romance between singles does blossom at the office, the wisest course is to take it slowly, get to know each other in a variety of circumstances away from work before getting deeply involved. If the affair breaks up, it still will hurt. But if, before starting, each partner has found that the other can be considerate and respectful, even under trying circumstances, there is a better chance that they could become friends again. One might even get a generous kick out of offering the other introductions to eligible single friends.

Anyone who is young and looking for a successful mate would do well to concentrate on prospective successes. Signs of future achievement are found in the person with high aptitudes, a good early track record and a consistent knack for making things turn out well. The prospective success may be a brilliant professional acquiring top credentials (Daphne's husband, Philip), an entrepreneurial mind who sees gaps and finds effective ways of filling them (Samantha's husband, Greg) or someone geared to rising strategically on an organizational ladder (Suzanne's husband, Doug Middleworth). Whichever it is, the marrier-up will need to strike a balance between being supportive to the achieving spouse and continuing his or her own independent growth. Like Greg's first wife (and Dan's and Wally's), clinging spouses and bitter, critical ones of both sexes often have been discarded after the budding achievers blossomed.

At a time when the news reports are filled with unemployment statistics and stories about dependable, experienced workers at every level who can't find jobs, suggestions about socially advantageous choices of occupation, location and focus may seem ironic. But even in the severe Depression of the 1930s, some investments prospered, some people made profits in business, built up professional practices, succeeded in cultural or entertainment fields, supported families and enjoyed material comforts. Even in a period of high unemployment some people get good jobs, find two jobs to work concurrently, find ways to have the training they need and engage in the activities they enjoy.

There are reshufflings in hard times. When a small business fails, the personal assets of its owner may be completely wiped out. When the failed business is big enough, the owner usually is able to protect a substantial part of his personal fortune. In a changing economy, some established businesses fade or assume new shapes. Marginal operations adapt or go under. New successes emerge.

No one can predict with absolute accuracy which enterprises or which individuals will gain prominence and profits and which ones will keep them. In discussing different ways that the workplace provides access to upwardly mobile matrimonial possibilities, I make no specific recommendations for individual readers. There are too many variables and no guarantees. My purpose has been to review the patterns, connections and attitudes that frequently have made such access possible.

# 8

## Playing Up

### Working at Play

People who are determined to improve their lot in life do not leave that improvement passively to hope and luck. They understand that betterment is not a one-shot operation. In the preceding chapter we considered some ways in which a person can change the nature, location or emphasis of his or her work in order to gain more exposure to privileged people. What applies to work applies to play. Almost all activities can be chosen and pursued with the same, purposeful focus as work.

Play does not necessarily mean something restful or frivolous. People sometimes report feeling that they are paid to "play" when the work they do engrosses them and allows them opportunities to use their imaginations, tackle chores that interest them, create their own projects, or choose the problems they want to solve. Artists who make a living at their art come to mind, but creativity is not limited to the arts. It can be found in business, science, the professions and service occupations.

Many creative people have no hobbies and spend little

time at traditional forms of recreation. They approach the mechanics of daily life as interesting situations with potential for imaginative handling. A clever hostess who mixes an assortment of guests in a way likely to produce stimulating conversation also finds it an absorbing pastime to mix several kinds of flatware, china and household objects in an unusual way for a notable table setting. A decorator, building new closets into her own dressing room and displeased with the look of available hardware, experiences a small triumph in devising a new kind of magnetic catch for the doors. A painter whose subject is flowers builds a greenhouse alongside the glass wall of his studio and cultivates his own models. Alexander Calder, the sculptor known for his large stabile and mobile metal compositions, fashioned kitchen utensils out of wire and rods and saw them used daily in his home. When Picasso boned a fish for lunch, he turned the skeleton into a piece of sculptural relief. My husband, whose paid work was the making of beautiful photographs, could not simply plant a garden around his house. He set to work breeding flowering plants for optimal growth and became so expert that, eventually, he introduced a whole new strain of delphinium, the Connecticut Yankee, into the world. Creative people enjoy keeping their minds at work most of the time, "playing" at ideas and possible outcomes.

Others, including many of the rich and upwardly mobile, choose as play recreational activities that offer tough challenges, opportunities for hard-won mastery or a sense of creative accomplishment. Consider the following: the disciplined physical power applied in skiing or diving; the coordination for conquest in football and chess; the stylized hand-to-hand combat of tennis; the stalking focus of hunting and its symbolic refinement in golf; the polite, regulated structure of competitive commerce in bridge; the ritualized sexual courtship of dancing; the interweaving of private effort and public display in fancy needlework, gourmet cooking, gardening or playing the piano; the earned mental expansion of studying Sanskrit or the history of philosophy. Being the kind of member of the audience who can discuss the play or concert or ballet knowledgeably later also requires attentive effort and learning in a particular frame of reference. These forms of "play" mirror the major serious issues of life: survival, protection of territory, conquest of enemies and appropriation of goods through strength or strategy, mating, provision of food and shelter, pondering the mysteries of existence, communicating ideas and emotions.

## The Hard Approach to A Soft Life

The rich are self-conscious about their reputedly easy lives. They traditionally send their children to camps that feature rugged, Spartan routines and accommodations and steer them into sports that encourage discipline, initiative, and cooperation with others. The display-oriented, New Money rich are an exception. They often use their children as a means of conspicuous consumption and insulate them with many layers of luxury goods and services.

The old rich and the aggressive, newly successful often choose for their own recreation challenging activities that keep their minds and bodies alert and fit. They can be found skillfully negotiating the tennis court, coordinating wind and halyard, guiding a horse over fences, shooting the rapids, exploring remote and rugged terrain on foot. They are likely to be knowledgeable in the technology and handling of cameras, telescopes, airplanes and racing cars, or in the breeding of specialized strains of plants and animals. They are drawn to advanced expertise on the esoteric, be it butterflies, stamps, porcelains or pre-Columbian rituals. Mastery of anything complex or difficult reinforces the sense of being entitled to privilege and power. Challenge keeps a person interested in being alive.

Among the rich, a poorer acquaintance's ability to share
their pleasure and skill in athletic and cultural pursuits can
form a basis for continuing a relationship. Unusual expertise
occasionally can provide the basis for starting a relationship.
But in the initial pursuit of that more privileged circle of
acquaintance, the pursuer's "play," the things he or she does
other than work for which he is paid, may not have much to
do with what is commonly thought of as recreation. "Play"
may consist of inconvenient logistical choices, taking care of
everyday chores and participating in recreation in out-of-the-
way locations and on awkward schedules chosen for their
potential exposure to certain groups of people. "Play" may
consist of serious educational activities, formal and informal,
from tennis lessons and antiques browsing to foreign language tutoring and music appreciation classes. A lot of time
may be spent learning about the major cultural areas and the
minor trivia with which the affluent are at home. The pursuer's "play" may have a lot to do with offering time in the
service of the artistic, intellectual, political and philanthropic
causes that interest the privileged.

## Play in Print

An aspiring mover-up who just wants to know the names
of the watering holes where the privileged can be found will
be better off compiling lists from recent issues of some publications I will suggest than paying attention to any names I
happen to mention as illustrations. While some places (like
New York's "21" and Antibes' Hotel du Cap) seem to go on
forever, fashions in chic hangouts for the affluent change
rapidly. What is new and what is "in" with various groups
turn up with regular reading of the magazines and newspapers that promote an upper-class image in dress, housing,
entertaining and cultural pursuits.

*Vogue, W, Town & Country, House & Garden, Bon Appetit,*

*Gourmet*, mention or feature resorts, spas and restaurants, along with proclaiming which books, movies, artworks, hemlines, window treatments and cocktail snacks are "in" each week or month or season. The small advertisements in the back pages of *The New Yorker* also can be used judiciously as guides to city hotels, country inns and little resorts that have acceptable cachet among the affluent, middle-brow intelligentsia. These are the people who believe that small size, tranquility and "good taste" are higher class than big, razzle-dazzle glitter. Some of the magazines geared to specific populations or locations, such as *The Washingtonian* or *Ebony*, offer information on who is important and what is "in." *GQ* does it for men of fashion. Magazines on the order of *New York* and *New West* offer splashy articles listing fashionable places, but their point of view is that of the striver trying to make it against difficult odds and not that of those who have been around comfortably for a while.

Studies of the kinds of homes in which a variety of better-than-well-off people actually live can be pursued in *House & Garden*, as well as in features that turn up in regional magazines and Sunday supplements. *Town & Country* often devotes an entire issue to one city or region, photographs members of prominent families in a style deliberately slanted to convey an old guard image, and lists the nitty gritty details of fashionable shops, restaurants, hairdressers and other services. As well as letting the reader know how much it is possible to pay for women's clothes, *Vogue* comments briefly on books, art, movies and restaurants, points out expensive new fads in travel and personal care, and photographs the fasionably celebrated at home.

*W*, the bi-weekly color tabloid that covers the tax deductible activities of the high-priced end of the rag trade (garment industry) and its best customers, occasionally shows men's clothes along with the usual display of women's, regularly reports on new fads, and does feature stories on the life styles of the fashion-connected Statustocracy who spend a lot of time crossing oceans in airplanes. *W* is the self-appointed arbiter for this set of what is "in" and "out" in menus, looks, watering holes and people. The food ideas, sensibly adapted, can be useful for the pursuer's own entertaining, as well as for recognizing what others in the network are serving. *Vogue* and *House & Garden* also offer menus and recipes with an upper-class orientation. *Antiques*, *Art in America* and other specialized arts magazines serve the serious collector or fan. Major institutions such as the Smithsonian have their own publications that offer the reader some shortcuts to becoming culturally informed.

No newspaper in the country equals *The New York Times* Style page and its related feature departments in providing specific information while setting a tone of class based on background and achievement, but every newspaper has at least one column that makes some reference to places where the affluent wine, dine, cavort and vacation. The *Washington Post* has on its natural beat some of the world's biggest movers and shakers. Papers like the *Miami Herald*, which maintains separate bureaus and publishes separate editions for each major locality within its circulation area, do thorough jobs on covering the social scene. The Social Registers of New York and other cities are primarily useful for getting the children of listed families into proper dancing classes, but they can be of some help to the social pursuer interested in learning names and genealogies.

When reading about goods and services that are fashionable among the successful, it is important to remember that the fields of soft news and paid promotion sometimes overlap. It is difficult to keep entirely separate the information a journalist receives from his own investigative efforts and private connections and those from public relations promotion sources. No matter what the source of information by the time a place is mentioned in print as fashionable, restless

Statustocrats are off elsewhere, to seek something more exclusive and undiscovered.

## Mixing

Many of the very rich still dine out primarily at private homes or clubs or at well-screened private parties in public places. For vacations they prefer private quarters: houses, compounds, boats. These can be owned, borrowed or rented. Pace Dollarson's niece, Holly, unmarried and living on trust funds from the estates of her Dollarson grandfather and her famous novelist mother, never stays at hotels. There is a prince with a chalet in Gstaad, a columnist with a flat in Knightsbridge, a countess with a *palazzo* on the Grand Canal, a banker with a *finca* west of Bogotá, a cabinet member with a house in Georgetown, all with guest rooms available for Holly, most with full-time domestic servants in attendance. While Holly may have to search the closets for clean sheets at the journalist's and bring in her own soap and breakfast food at the *palazzo*, the banker is likely to send the Lear jet to fetch her from her previous stopover. These people are part of a network of school friends, family friends, cousins, aunts, extended family in-laws, admirers, mother's admirers and other connections accumulated since Holly's birth.

Betts Bucksborn's family still collectively maintains the "camp" in the Adirondacks. All over the country there are family enclaves on secluded estates, beach compounds, private lakes and islands, hunting lodges, remote ranches, and old-time summer plantations. The rich without family compounds buy or rent mountain or seaside houses in heavily guarded communities accessible only by boat or private road beyond a manned gate. Admission to these is only as an invited guest or as an employee.

However, anyone who is relentlessly curious and can afford transportation, tips and room rates that seldom dip below six hundred dollars a day can check into the best hotels on St. Martin, on the Costa Smeralda, at Klosters, in Kenya, or the no-nonsense glamour spas like the Ashram in California. On the beach, in the dining room, at the ski lift or the door to the treatment room, the curious may see the rich, the famous and the royal-blooded. But they may never have a chance to talk to them. Most of the rich do not travel alone. If an outsider were to manage to fall into conversation or even pick up a tennis game, he or she would have to come up with something singularly striking in order to warrant a continuing acquaintance. An act of courageous rescue could make the outsider more memorable, but such opportunities do not arrive often.

Some of the smaller, expensive, one-sex spas (such as Maine Chance in Arizona, the Phoenix in Texas, the Greenhouse and the Golden Door) offer more opportunity for repeated contact with fellow guests at the common dining table and the exercise classes. Cordial relationships often spring up during the stay, but guests lead busy lives in scattered parts of the country. The odds are high against being able to sustain such a relationship and use it in network building.

## *Organized Mixing*

In many large cities and affluent suburbs there are clubs for singles where eligibility for membership is based on an occupation of career caliber or an income above a certain minimum. These organizationa advertise locally, in publications geared to the economic and career groups they want to attract. A prototype is the Millionaire's Club of Newport Beach, California. The idea is to offer busy, successful singles appropriate opportunities for meeting each other. These are profit-making operations and the fees are high. Activities and services range from sports and health-related facilities through parties, dances, travel and computer dating to group therapy and counseling sessions.

In many busy industrial and commercial cities, and in the

suburbs of the biggest ones, there are luxury housing com-
plexes that feature small apartments and an array of recreational facilities designed to accommodate prosperous, working
singles. Many of the singles who choose to live in these com-
plexes or join these clubs claim that they are too new in town
and too busy with their work to know where to go or to have
time to meet people and develop social networks on their
own. But many of them also suffer from the negative club
membership syndrome described in Chapter 5: They can't
imagine wanting to get involved with the sort of person who
would express interest in them. Here, as in other singles
settings, many of the people who claim and believe that they
are looking for a "meaningful" and continuing relationship
really are terrified of getting close to anyone.

## Volunteering

In play, as in work, useful networks develop more easily
when there is opportunity for repeated visibility and contact.
A major, continuing activity available to almost everyone is
volunteer work in philanthropic and cultural organizations.
There are many different types. The possibilities vary according to region and community and according to age, sex,
abilities and interests of the prospective volunteers. Any functioning human being with a little spare time has something
to offer to some organization. Through offering that something, a person has a chance to get to know people who might
never have turned up in his or her other usual haunts.

All this takes time, of course, and someone carrying twelve
college credits while working forty hours a week may have
to concentrate on those two parts of the plan for upward
mobility and forgo this one for a while. But anyone who has
time for evenings of TV or phone conversations or barstool
warming, or who finds that most of Sunday just goes by
"doing nothing," has time for regular volunteer work with
nonprofit organizations.

Rich people, and those who have influential access to the rich, serve on the boards of non-profit organizations. In some upper-class families, seats on certain boards get handed down from one generation to the next. (The Bucksborns are family service, the Van Lucres the hospital, the Dollarsons the art museum.) Often a distinguished ancestor was one of the founders. A few board members may be there because of expertise in a particular field, but the primary function of a board is to keep that organization operating soundly in its policies, programs and financing. Fund raising is the major responsibility of the board. The rich board members and their companies make substantial contributions, and they have the kind of leverage in the community that gets others to come through handsomely, too.

Most of these organizations also depend on several kinds of less exalted volunteer activities. These are frequently divided into committees, which are most likely to be led by rich or upper-class people. Their families, too, have a history with the organization, or they have leisure time to give, or they work at the kinds of jobs from which they can free time. They belong to the Useful Money rich, who are trained to engage responsibly in activities that are of benefit to the community. Volunteer work is one of those expected obligations, as well as a way of maintaining a kind of respectable visibility within their own circles. Anyone who becomes a volunteer worker for a philanthropic organization and serves on one or more of its committees has some chance of coming into regular contact with some of these well connected volunteers.

## Philanthropy

Philanthropies that use the services of volunteers deal with poverty, social and environmental problems, disease, physical and mental handicaps, and children or adults who have been mistreated in various ways. Each region has its own possibilities for volunteer work: school and tutoring programs, aid to unwed mothers, athletic coaching and other youth activities, organizations for runaways, the homeless and the aged, emergency disaster relief and programs for the beautification and increased safety of the community.

While Old Money volunteers often pick their philanthropic involvements on the basis of family history (many are active in family foundations that focus on particular areas), there are still subtle shifts in fashion for volunteer service. Certain diseases, like cancer, began to receive more respectable public support for care and research once the scientific evidence indicated strongly that contracting it had nothing to do with immoral behavior or bad living habits. On the other hand, some fiscally solid citizens serve actively with prison reform and drug rehabilitation organizations.

Most hospitals offer opportunities for volunteer work. If there is a choice in the community, the astute candidate for moving up picks the hospital where the upper classes go for medical treatment. That is where members of those classes will also volunteer and serve on the board. It is also where the medical staff is likely to be more affluent and socially mobile. There is a philanthropy for almost every disease. Many have more than one organization at both local and national levels. Some philanthropies offer more rewards than others to their volunteers and more gatherings at which volunteers and board members can meet each other.

In some organizations the volunteer work is routine and isolated. In others it includes shared activities or dealing with the public and board members in preparing fund raising events. To find out what sort of activities each organization offers, the astute mover-up checks newspapers for reports of theater and concert benefits, dinner dances, auctions, house tours, sports competitions and other fundraisers. A prospective volunteer can call organizations and ask them directly about the range of volunteer activities. The person planning his or her own kind of volunteer campaign checks the mailbox for solicitations. A small contribution will bring the organization's newsletter, if it has one. If it shows volunteers engaged in public and social activities, or numbers of committee members meeting and working together frequently, those are clues that the organization may offer superior opportunities for network building in exchange for time and effort spent on its behalf. Some communities have an information clearing house for volunteer activities. Even the Yellow Pages of the telephone book give clues under the heading, "Associations."

## Commitment

Some organizations make better use of the volunteer's specific abilities and appeal to the individual's self-esteem more than others. Trial and error sampling is the method many people use to find out which is which. There is nothing wrong with moving around so long as the volunteer doesn't promise too much at the beginning and fulfills whatever commitment he or she has made before leaving.

The local newspapers, the organizations' newsletters, letterheads and fund appeals give some idea of where the most prominent people serve. The process of network building is not quick. Once the aspiring mover-up picks a reasonably satisfactory organization, he or she may spend a lot of time there. It happens from time to time that people who have volunteered primarily out of selfish interest have become very pleased with themselves for taking on the commitment and have developed pride in their service and accomplishments.

People who get involved and enthusiastic in their volunteer work have some likelihood of doing an outstanding job. When they do, they usually get recognition for it. They become more visible. It sometimes follows that more people seek them out, want to know them. Of course, good work is seldom enough. Developing a social network also requires perpetual curiosity, friendly, outgoing behavior, willingness to take some risks, be rejected, try again, not hold grudges and keep track of who is related to whom and who cares about what.

Sometimes volunteer tasks can be frivolous and the commitment superficial. In my early single days in New York, whenever we had no "dates," a friend and I spent Saturday evenings at the old Squadron A Armory watching the indoor polo games. We were both excellent riders and loved almost anything that had to do with horses. The public was welcome at the polo games for a small admission fee that did not strain the tight budgets dictated by our modest salaries. Gradually we met some other regulars, who were members or friends of members of the polo club. One of them asked—actually begged—me to help sell tickets for a fund-raising event to support research on a disease. My volunteer stint consisted of sitting for several hours at lunch and cocktail time at a table just inside the entrance to a fashionable midtown watering hole. As instructed, I wore a polo helmet, which attracted enough attention to allow me to repeat my ticket-selling pitch frequently.

As a gesture of thanks, a committee co-chairman called and invited me to a party at a rambling Fifth Avenue apartment overlooking the park and furnished casually with the minor but good antiques and art works that the aristocratically educated upper classes take for granted as basic supplies. The guests were a fairly young and lively group: one or two European titles making their way in New York business and public relations, two or three known theater people, one destined to become rich and famous in the movies, an assortment of people in publishing, brokerage, banking and pastimes engaged in by those who do not have to start from scratch to make their way in the world. This room did not represent the richest, most conservative aristocracy, but it offered some links to that echelon, and it contained plenty of high-powered success and privilege. I had never met any of these people before, I knew—and only slightly—just one other person who had a comparable apartment and array of friends. I was there only because in the course of pursuing a genuine interest, I had reluctantly agreed to spend a few hours looking slightly ridiculous in the name of a worthy cause.

Some of my *How to Marry Money* students have groaned when I mentioned volunteer work. They complain that it's useless, the rich volunteers are all older women and married men (or married women and men past retirement age), or all the volunteers are poor schemers like themselves. The committed mover-up remembers that the goal is to build a network, not just to look for that one eligible member of the opposite sex. The idea is to make friends—friends who will introduce the ambitious volunteer to their friends and family members until, somewhere in that expanding circle, a potential mate turns up. In the meantime the volunteer gets a chance to see how it feels to think of himself or herself as an active, valued, connected member of the community.

## Culture and Politics

The philanthropies dedicated to improving social conditions and curing disease do not offer the only opportunities for volunteer work. Many different kinds of cultural organizations also welcome unpaid assistance and have similar structures of boards and committees. These include: symphony orchestras, opera houses, dance companies, regional theaters, art museums, natural history museums, historical societies, botanical gardens, zoological societies, public broadcasting stations, societies for architectural preservation and societies for the preservation of endangered species. Most of these need volunteers to staff fund-raising benefits and opening receptions, work in gift and book shops, help out in the membership offices, and perform clerical tasks. Some use the more sophisticated skills of volunteers for auxiliary curatorial assistance, teaching and guided tours. The selection process here for the prospective volunteer is the same as for other kinds of philanthropies: observation and trial and error.

There are always differences of region and community, but, traditionally, the musical organizations have been the favorites of the conservative Old Money rich. Politically, music is the safest art form. Pianos, violins and oboes don't come out with radical words. The usual opera repertoire refers to the romantic past and does so in languages few members of the audience understand.

Big New Money often turns up actively involved in art museums and makes huge contributions to them. In contemporary art, given to rapid, Messianic waves of fashion, bold New Money mixes most easily with the brave but baffled Old. Among collectors Old and New, critical judgment becomes a "talent" valued competitively in its own right. Lending from one's collection for exhibitions and having one's gifts of art works accepted for the permanent collections of major museums becomes the quintessential recognition for this talent of discernment.

In many communities there are also amateur performing organizations with high standards. They may be orchestras, choruses, drama clubs, or light opera companies. They may have been started by old society families, but they sometimes welcome new members with specific skills or the willingness to paint scenery, print programs or sell tickets. The determined joiner can track down their activities through the same sources as the philanthropies or by keeping abreast of all announcements of performances in the local media. Even if they are snobbish and difficult to join, they want audiences. For the mover-up who gets in, they provide another chance for the kind of exposure that can lead to enlarging the social network.

Political campaigns also offer many opportunities for volunteering. For anyone reluctant to make a long-term commitment, a political campaign offers the advantage of a built-in termination date. Campaigns are conducted at all levels—municipal, county, state, national—for every kind of office. Skills required of volunteers can range from licking envelopes to writing television commercials. Even though Nelson Rockefeller began to become noticeably involved with his future second wife, Happy, after she went to work for one of his political campaigns, the general rule for serious movers-up is to avoid flirting with the candidate. Political candidates become "stars," at least for a while, and fall prey to the groupie syndrome of easy sex: easily gotten, easily forgotten. However, since even the most radically egalitarian reform candidate needs people with money to fund and support his campaign, the astute movers-up look to the finance committee of a campaign as an obvious good place for finding out who the powerful money people are and for meeting them. Most finance committee members are likely to come from backgrounds or occupations associated with money.

The newcomer may not find all committees open to him or to her at first. Any task that allows the new arrival to meet people and keep his or her eyes open is good for a start. Low level experience on one campaign can make the volunteer eligible next time for a post that offers closer proximity to the kinds of people he or she has in mind.

## Persistence

In any of a mover-up's volunteer activities, patience, persistence, and an eye for ways of distinguishing oneself are important. Networks for upward social mobility usually do not evolve quickly. The rich people the mover-up wants to know had the advantage of growing up with these networks. Some of the people the new volunteer meets for the first time will have known each other all their lives. There is comfort in familiarity, in a history, in being able to say, "Remember when...?" It is possible for newcomers to develop histories with some of these people, too, but it can take several years before they look back and laugh with a fellow committee member about the time they mixed up all the place cards or didn't remember the candidate. It is that kind of history of shared experience that changes people from strangers into comfortable familiars. What moves them further into being friends, and friends who are willing to share their other friends, depends on what each individual needs and on what the outsider, from his or her energy, interests, experience and sensitivity, has to offer.

In choosing volunteer work the newcomer can spend some time sampling, looking around, making changes and taking on new activities. But for serious network building, most determined movers-up try to find at least one organization that interests them enough to stay with it for two years or more. It takes that long to become known and to know which connections really turn out to matter. They find it essential to select an activity or organization to which they can bring some enthusiasm. Feeling resentful about wasting one's time seldom fosters the kind of participation that earns recognition and friends or that makes the mover-up appealing when eligible marital material turns up.

## Affluent Orientations

While the workplace and sustained volunteer activities offer most people the best opportunities for building an upwardly mobile network and finding a worthwhile mate, other areas of life offer possibilities for reorientation. Two relatively young people who are expert at this kind of orientation are Jack Nimblestriver and Jill Upperclimbing. They are both attractive and personable, though not dazzlers. They are not rich. Each has specialized knowledge and skills. Jill is always in demand as a tennis partner. Jack sings with an amateur light opera company. He is a crackerjack crew member on any sailing vessel. Jill usually knows who the hottest new artists are before they become expensive. Between them they have a great deal of dedicated experience in testing various social ladders. Each might have married up to a great deal of money several times but each believes that an even more suitable marital partner will turn up just beyond the next rung. In the meantime, they keep in practice.

Jack buys at least a few of his groceries or delicacies regularly at food stores that cater to the group of people he wants eventually to join. Jill patronizes a fashionable hairdresser and, to compensate for the higher cost, goes less often than she might choose. She knows that such places usually charge higher fees for the services of owners and famous operators, so she schedules her appointments with other employees who perform the same services in the same environment at lower cost. Both Jack and Jill frequent the stores where several categories of rich people shop. They repeatedly familiarize themselves with the look, feel and prices of quality merchandise so that they can recognize it elsewhere. When they see someone dressed in it regularly or find someone's home and table furnished in it, they not only recognize money but they also can identify the type of money.

Religion has meaning for Jill. She has found it possible to be just as devout at a society church (or synagogue if she were Jewish) as at one where the congregation is middle or working class. She studies the dress and manners of her fellow worshipers. She has explored volunteer activities through the church. She has found that some congregations sponsor a broad array of community-oriented activities, while others specialize in offering introspective, self-help groups. She has learned through experience that the former attract the kinds of committee members she wants to meet in any volunteer activity. The latter tend to attract people who are floundering about the edges of life and need to do a lot of growing before they can offer much to anyone else.

Jack has considered carefully where he lives. He discovered that it would cost him about the same to have a tiny apartment in or near an upper-class neighborhood as a spacious apartment or house in a working-class neighborhood. He took the tiny one in the upper-class area. He is closer to the kind of environment in which he plans to be permanently at home. He also figured out that it is less expensive to decorate and maintain a small place than a large one. Both he and Jill find it important to have a home to which they can bring new, privileged friends without embarrassment. Both have found that the newer the money and the more Snob the strivings of their privileged friends, the more the particulars of the dwellings will matter to them.

An exception to the rule of small quarters in the best neighborhood occurs when there is access to large or interesting space in an old area inhabited by artists or being reclaimed by other pioneers with esthetic and social standards. This could be a loft district, a neighborhood of Victorian working-class houses, an abandoned mill, church, firehouse or bank building or a broken down commercial fishing pier. Often, artists move to such neighborhoods first, for cheap space, and improve the property for their own use. Or middle-class professionals buy salvageable, rundown housing that they can afford, and they restore it. Then gentrification sets in. The neighborhood becomes attractive to affluent and stylish people and the prices rise. Jill is now exploring a "new" loft neighborhood just opening up to residential conversion.

Jack is comfortable dropping into a bar after work. He lives in the sort of community where executives and bigger money professionals have favorite bars where they stop on the way home. He sees no harm in being a regular at one, provided he drinks moderately and limits his stays to less than an hour. His program requires more of him than hanging around as a barfly. However, some of the conversations he has overheard at the bar have enlarged his frame of reference. Once or twice, he has expanded his network through acquaintance with some of the other regulars.

Jill likes to be familiar with the expensive new restaurants in town. When she is picking up the check, she patronizes them for lunch rather than dinner as the lunch menu is cheaper. She has found that, if she is well-dressed, tips slightly more than twenty percent, keeps a straight face and offers no apologies, she can order a dozen oysters and a Perrier as her entire lunch and be accepted as simply another affluent dieter or food faddist.

If a new health club with elaborate facilities is attracting the locally affluent, Jill takes a short-term membership and looks around. If he hears that the Wall Street crowd has taken up skeet shooting at public galleries to work off their tensions, Jack joins them. Jack and Jill rub elbows a lot—and not just with each other. They go to openings at art galleries and make the regular Saturday rounds. They go to art and antique auctions and to all the major shows.

## Concentration

Jack Nimblestriver and Jill Upperclimbing know that none of the situations listed in the last eight paragraphs is in itself a likely opportunity for meeting a rich mate. They use them as superficial orientation to the kind of life style to which they hope to become accustomed. Jack and Jill also have acquired skills and knowledge in areas that are traditionally of interest to the kinds of richer, better-connected people that interest them. In becoming very well informed and skilled in tennis, contemporary art, sailing, light opera and other specialties, Jack and Jill have moved to a more serious level of acclimatization. They also have filled their lives with challenging and enjoyable pursuits. Interests like these are used as bonds to sustain acquaintance after a mover-up meets privileged people. Occasionally, if they develop sufficient knowledge, well-informed movers-up are singled out as expert amateurs who are sought after for refined judgment or informed companionship.

For example, art, antiques, and architectural preservation long have been interests of the rich. There is comfort and safety in the great works of the past. A settled, upper-class background with a continuing supply of money is more conducive to this attitude than a background of struggle, upheaval and poverty. Observers of urban renewal report that people in working-class neighborhoods want new looks and new materials. It usually takes several generations of affluence and higher education to develop an interest in the old. Artists and intellectuals renovate Victorian factory workers' row houses with fidelity to old brick and clapboard construction. Factory workers are more interested in economical, new-looking, low-maintenance structures.

Another appeal of art and fine objects is that appreciating beauty with discernment can imply almost as much talent as creating it. Jack has an uncle, August Nimblestriver, who became well enough informed on Chinese cloisonné—or was it Maybeck houses?—to write about them occasionally for a specialized magazine and to lecture at small club meetings. His name became known to affluent people who shared the same interest. Since he was also an agreeable companion, he was invited from time to time on all-expense-paid trips to track down architectural finds and rare bibelots.

The rich care about preserving green, open space and elegant old buildings, particularly in the communities in which their own homes are located. Becoming an expert on environmental issues and preservation can make a mover-up sympathetic and useful on one of their committees. Horticulture, landscaping, raising plants in environments for which they were not originally intended are popular pastimes of the rich.

They are also traditionally fond of animals. They get concerned about species facing extinction and form committees to save them. They raise sporting dogs for tracking and retrieving the prey they hunt. They like house pets from uncommon breeds: Welsh Corgi, Dandie Dinmont, Wirehaired Dachshund, Jack Russell Terrier. The Irish Wolfhounds and Rhodesian Ridgebacks are for large country estates, where peacocks may turn up on the lawn and buffalo in the pasture. Sometimes they breed and show dogs. They often are open to appreciative comments and expert advice.

They breed cattle and horses, too. They ride to hounds (foxhunt), show saddle horses and Arabians, have racing stables. Beagling (rabbit hunting) is done on foot but with the same ritual as foxhunting. Despite periodic rumors of popularization, polo retains its limited, upper-class appeal, because the expense in acquiring, maintaining and transporting trained ponies limits participation to those with money, and the vast space required to play polo limits its practical possibilities as a spectator sport. Racing sailing is also an activity that requires money and remains popular with many of those who have it. Some rich people enjoy owning professional baseball and football teams.

Different aspirants for moving up and marrying up use the recreation of the privileged in different ways to make contact and maintain connections. Long-term activities not necessarily recreational in nature but geared for recognition and acceptance by the desired social group, as well as for personal satisfaction, remain my main recommendation for the "play" of those who really want to improve their lot. The rearing and education of the well-to-do and well-connected allow them to become informed on a great many matters in which they never participate themselves. When someone trains deliberately for a move up, concentrated effort often is required in order to catch up on the information that will permit the newcomer to be comfortable among the privileged.

As the upwardly mobile networks expand, realistic assessment of self and the desired environment are also needed in order to decide which subjects and activities to pursue in depth.

# Part III

---

# Strategies

## Assessing the field
## and the players

It seems crazy but you must believe
There's nothing calculated, nothing planned
Please forgive me if I seem naïve
I would never want to force your hand
But please understand
I'd be good for you...

Tim Rice
*Evita*

# 9

## Sleuths, Gossips and Researchers

### The Art of Pursuit

The people who are determined to marry up may work at other jobs, but every choice they make is dictated by the priority of maintaining the right connections in order to have the right opportunity at the right time to meet a prospective mate. Some read obituaries to spot widows and widowers of an appropriate age and within reach of their networks. Some cultivate friendships with divorce lawyers, hoping to get hot tips on people about to become available. Some of the younger ones rely on their own or their parents' well-placed friends in finance, academia, business and the professions, to point out young singles with brilliant futures. There are many different ways in which to use a network.

Hattie was a well-connected woman of comfortable means, married for forty-two years. She was over sixty-five when her husband died. She decided that she preferred being married. Even though the odds were not statistically in her favor she set out to marry again. Hattie always had been active in an extensive circle of social acquaintances. Now, she used the gossip in that network to keep her alert for signs that married women in her set had become seriously ill. If there were frequently cancelled social engagements, unpleasantly altered appearance, changes in customary travel and other routine, time spent in hospitals for tests, she would start paying special attention to that couple. She would make frequent calls and visits.

If it turned out that the wife had a terminal illness, Hattie would come up with recommendations for specialists and private duty nurses. She would send thoughtful gifts to hospital and sickroom and give tactful assistance to the husband in keeping domestic arrangements running smoothly. As the end neared, Hattie appointed herself the buffer between intrusions from the community and the couple's pain and grief. By the time the wife died, the widower couldn't imagine how he ever had lived without Hattie. Unfortunately, she was operating in a high-risk age bracket. The widowers had a tendency to die before she could get them to the altar. But after several tries, she latched on to a healthy survivor and took good care of him. The marriage was a contented one.

Barbara, the woman who spent money on the things that showed and carried the pots and pans back and forth, was also widowed, but in her forties. Barbara had artistic pretensions, and her artist friends (mostly poor bohemians and creative homosexuals) added a certain amusing dash to her solid businessman husband's social life. When he died she determined to remarry. Assessing the field, she realized that the kinds of men who marry and who pull their financial weight in a marriage did not exist among her bohemian friends. In fact, her association with them tended to make her more traditional acquaintances think she was not interested in a conventional marriage.

So Barbara dropped all her artist friends. She became a relentless joiner of committees and giver of proper dinner parties for married couples. She always found some respectable looking man to attend alone and balance the table. She always managed, discreetly, to let the women know that there was something unsuitable about the man as husband material. The message was clear. Barbara was to be invited to dinner, and an eligible, unattached man was to be provided as a dinner partner. She gave two or three dinner parties for every return invitation, but the return invitations did arrive. At one of these dinners, a man of appropriate age and substance, recently divorced from an indifferent wife, turned up ready for a relationship with a caring woman. After settling into her new marriage, Barbara began to invite some of her old bohemian friends again to spice up her larger parties.

Barbara and Hattie researched their own situations through personal observation and gossip. They figured out where the potential mates might turn up. They focused their efforts on those areas, and they persisted through many rounds of disappointment. They may sound callous and given to treating people as interchangeable figures in a design. Yet Barbara and Hattie both were capable of warmth, affection and devotion. So was the equally calculating Daphne, our diligent and successful pursuer of the rising young professional man.

When Cal Bucksborn, the aristocratic heir to a substantial family business, proposed to the equally aristocratic Betts, he found her no more or less appealing personally than three or four other single women he knew. He simply found that her particular kind of educated, upper-class background had prepared her the most suitably to be a full participant in the kind of life he expected to lead. Betts' reasons for accepting Cal were quite similar. Both had brief, discreet affairs in the first ten years of their marriage. These were taken on lightly, for a bit of variety, and were abandoned before they could interfere with the spouses' basic loyalty or liking for each other.

Cal, Betts, Daphne, Barbara and Hattie all represent reasonably decent, practical survivors. They were willing, when

necessary, to sacrifice the short-term indulgence of impracti-
cal whims for the long-term fulfillment of needs they took
seriously. They decided that the affection and devotion they
had to offer would fare better if it were directed to people
who could, in one way or another, enhance their positions
in the world. If they had to, they were willing to make coldly
logical choices and follow through with dauntless perserver-
ance,as Barbara and Hattie did, in order to achieve their goals.

## Curiosity

One of the most important tools for acquiring information
of any kind is curiosity. In the course of developing networks
productively, the would-be marrier-up has to acquire and
exercise a tremendous amount of it. Curiosity means thinking
in questions and finding answers. There are two questions
to keep in mind at all times. They are: Who is the richest,
most privileged person in this room? and: What does he—
or she—want that he does not have now?

Curiosity is a quality of mind, a habit, that can be culti-
vated, of thinking up questions about everything one sees
and hears. The truly curious never simply look at a person.
As they look, questions begin popping into their heads. Is
that a runner's stoop or a swimmer's stretch? Is there a name
for that haircut? Are those shoes Bally or Church or Flor-
sheim? Is there a monogram on his shirt? Is her jacket cashmere or a synthetic combination? Could the pearls be real?
Where do those "r's" come from? And the scar on the finger?
Does "we" mean a spouse, a child, a friend, an associate?
What TV star does he remind me of? What politician? What
person I know?

Are they talking about a party for Johnny Bench or Johnny
Carson? Do they mean Pauline de Rothschild or Pauline Tri-
gère? What's the note she's folding into her pocket? What's
the letterhead? Could he be related to—work with, live near,
go to school with—anyone I know? What is her favorite food?

Sport? Season? Does he belong to a club? Where does her family come from? Where is he going? Is he comfortable here? What would make her smile? Does he find this view refreshing? How long has she known those people? What does he think of municipals? Commodities? The new tax legislation? What kind of room did she sleep in as a child? Did he eat dinner with his parents when he was little? Who was her first friend? What secret vices would he confess to at the dinner table? What is his major ambition? His ideal woman? What is her idea of a perfect holiday? A sad moment? A triumph? Who is the most interesting person he knows?

Jack Nimblestriver and Jill Upperclimbing practice this kind of speculation everywhere: waiting for a bus or an elevator, in a line at the supermarket, the bank or the airline check-in counter. At a cocktail party or a dinner table, a break in work or a meeting, any situation in which there is a new person. The more homework they have done about the world they want to live in, the better informed they have made themselves—the less likely they are to embarrass themselves with completely ignorant or redundant questions. ("Who's the artist in the house?" when asked on entering a living room full of Surrealist and abstract paintings is likely to imply that the questioner comes from a background where the only art was on the insurance company calendar.) However, so long as they are pleasant, don't insist anxiously on getting answers, do pay attention to the replies they are given, and are willing to respond, briefly, lightly, to questions in return, their curiosity is most likely to be perceived as a part of a lively, outgoing, interested personality.

Some of the questions that arise should remain unasked, however, formed only in one's mind as an investigation to pursue obliquely and over a period of time. These have to do with hard financial facts, scandals, humiliations and other sticky situations in family and business dealings. Jill will ask what gallery represents the artist or who designed the bracelet, but not how much the painting or the diamonds cost. If

she's dealing with the kind of person who wants her to know
how much he can spend, he'll tell her what he paid for things
without being asked. Some of these questions can be asked,
delicately, of selected third parties with whom Jill has established a gossip relationship.

It seldom serves the marrier-up's purpose to ask someone
directly if he or she is rich, although if tossed off in an assured
and casual way at the right time, the question or its answer
can be disarming. If Jack meets someone with a familiar-
sounding name, he certainly can ask if he is a mining Moneywell or a banking Moneywell, a clothing Flushberth or a
building Fluschbirth, particularly if he can refer with knowledge, however superficial, to some member of the other family. So long as the situation is not an invasion of privacy,
people usually are pleased to be recognized and to be associated, respectfully, with fame and prosperity. But no one
likes to be grilled about his holdings, his business complications, his plans. Curiosity without insistence is a welcome
quality in a person who comes across as interested and well-
informed.

Anyone who sets out to marry up not only has to ask a
great many questions, he or she also has to remember a great
many answers. Jill Upperclimbing knows where to get hold
of information quickly, so she does not have to keep it all in
her head. Jill has set up a cross-indexed reference file that
lists all sorts of services, odd facts and special information
that might turn out to be of use in the circles in which she
wants to travel. Often, the concentration that goes into putting together an organized file and keeping it up to date has
a startling way of improving one's memory.

## Utility

One way that Jill makes herself interesting to others is by
coming up with specific bits of trivia, such as what the best

two dishes are supposed to be at the new Indonesian restaurant downtown or at Comme Chez Soi in Brussels or La Griglia d'Oro in Bologna; which ballets are being performed, and how well, by the visiting company; how to get to the private parking for the stadium; what the governor's wife's funny faux-pas was at the reception; the name of the architect of the local house commonly attributed to Frank Lloyd Wright, the differences between a Shang and a Chou dynasty bronze.

Jack Nimblestriver realized he had become socially useful to himself when he began to remember names and connections, when his curiosity became automatic and there was a steady increase in his ability to store away information and let the associations emerge at the appropriate times. Curiosity means following all leads to new information and new opportunities. It means exploring, at least briefly, everything that might be of interest or of use. It means accepting all invitations to every event that might include the kinds of people one wants to meet or the kinds of information one wants to acquire. It means learning to keep one's options open. Jack never sits down at a cocktail party unless he is talking to someone absolutely fascinating and has already checked out the rest of the guests. At a meeting, Jack hovers until he can pick a seat next to someone he would like to know. He covers a lot of territory by having a good excuse ready to leave any gathering early and go on to the next one. In ambitious and mobile circles, people are not insulted. Being in demand makes Jack more desirable, and they are flattered that he fit them in.

Jill has expanded her investigations to extending invitations. Competitive people usually are curious enough to accept an invitation to a gathering at a newly met person's home once. If the other guests or the setting prove interesting, offer new connections, or conversational anecdotes on which to dine out elsewhere, the new guests may reciprocate. One way to provide something most new acquaintances value is to use Wendy's technique and offer interesting and high status people a chance to meet each other.

A young man named Martin evolved a high-volume variation. Through his work he had access to some famous names and some power brokers for the would-be famous. Wherever he went, he dropped tantalizing references to these connections. His method of entertaining was to invite thirty or forty people in for drinks at 10 P.M. Drinks, and nothing else, were served. But everyone knew that he also had invited five people in for dinner earlier in the evening. Curiosity was piqued. Who was invited for dinner? Why? What did other people have to do to get invited? His small living room was always packed at ten o'clock with the curious and potentially useful. His mail was stuffed with invitations.

## Snooping and Trading

Sometimes the seeker of worthwhile new connections needs help in getting questions answered. One of the best general sources is gossip. One of the world's favorite pastimes is talking about people, offering speculation and judgments. People like to get information through gossip, but they also like to show how smart they are. They will sometimes reveal a lot in the process. At work and play, the determined seeker is sure to make friends with the best gossips. Their information is not accurate, but it gives the seeker leads to follow up later. In exchange for the tiniest morsels and a few questions, an astute seeker often picks up gems.

### Example 1

SEEKER: When I helped Mrs. Cashworth take the posters out, she said she'd invite us to lunch soon. There was a blond man waiting in the car—not the chauffeur. Was that her husband?

GOSSIP: Her husband is completely bald. What did he look like?

SEEKER: Sort of athletic.

GOSSIP: Hooked nose? Tall? Eyes close together? That's Teddy, her walker. *(A walker is a presentable, safe man, often homosexual, who accompanies a fashionable society matron to activities for which her husband is not appropriate or available.)*

SEEKER: I don't think so. I think he was sort of snub-nosed. And short.

GOSSIP: Could be her brother. Her half-brother. The art dealer.

SEEKER: Is *he* married?

GOSSIP: Divorced. His wife ran off with one of his sculptors.

SEEKER: Where is his gallery?

*Example 2*

SEEKER: I haven't seen that woman in the big horn rims before. What department is she in?

GOSSIP: That's Pushwilling's wife. They're separated, but she turns up sometimes. Tears herself away from the horse farm for state occasions. Less and less, though.

SEEKER: I thought he went for flashier types.

GOSSIP: He does. But she's a Wealthington.

SEEKER: Which branch?

GOSSIP: Only one I know of. The utilities people.

SEEKER: What kind of horses does she raise?

GOSSIP: Thoroughbreds. Racing.

SEEKER: I read something fascinating recently about the diet of thoroughbreds. Excuse me...

In other situations, being cordial and chatty over a period of time with the doorman, the pharmacy clerk, the liquor store clerk, the manicurist, the veterinarian's secretary, the mailman, the receptionist, the caterer's waitress, any of the service people in the places the seeker of information frequents, can produce tidbits that fill in important pieces in a profile of potentially available affluence and connections. It is useful to know not only who is affluent in that particular environment, but also what that person may need that an adaptable and resourceful human being like the seeker might supply or help to locate. Most service people like to let off a discreet bit of steam from time to time. If they feel the listener is sympathetic, not likely to complain about them, and not a stranger casing the premises for a burglary, they may say a lot. The trick is never to press them and never to seem too eager.

Even if the information-seeker does not live there, but visits regularly or walks a dog on the block every day, he or she becomes familiar. Dogwalking in a neighborhood of high-density population is a wonderful way to become acquainted with many details in the lives of the inhabitants. In an affluent neighborhood, a person standing alone in one spot on the sidewalk for any length of time is suspicious. A person standing at the end of the leash, waiting for a dog to finish sniffing and make up its mind, is just part of the scenery. In certain neighborhoods a detailed gossip network develops among the dogwalkers. Less frequently a social network develops.

The tendency for people to want to appear in the know can be used for perfecting the technique of glossing. In sociological parlance, "glossing" is a technique for seeking information by pretending to offer it. The glosser begins a statement that appears to be leading up to information which, in fact, he wants his listener to supply. At the critical moment he pauses and allows his listener to complete the statement.

GLOSSER: (*At a benefit cocktail party*) Sally is so clever about her little hideaways. You'd be surprised how many people think there's only this apartment and the Pound Ridge house. (*Pauses, looks around warily*)
FEEDER: Oh, the flat in Eaton Square is the only one that amounts to much. Vail and St. Martin's are just crash pads for Tim and the kids.

GLOSSER: (*Mysterious smile and shrug*)

FEEDER: Of course, her studio on Franklin Street is where the action is.

GLOSSER: (*Conspiratorial laugh*)

The glosser has never met the hostess before this evening, but he has heard about her, or read about her in *W* or in the style and culture pages or the gossip columns. He has just acquired four specific pieces of information about her that he did not have at the beginning of the conversation. And he has acquired it by assuming a position of ease and allowing the person with whom he was speaking to show off. In glossing, as distinguished from gossiping, the seeker really has no information to offer and asks no direct questions. Not everyone will fall for the technique. The glosser may have to live with being considered absentminded, vague or downright nosy, but the method can be useful. Sometimes it succeeds and turns up valuable nuggets about a person's wealth, location, marital status or personal preferences.

## Hidden Connections

Many of the people now interested in moving up through marriage and other strategies would do well to make a careful review of the old resources they have abandoned or forgotten a long time ago. The Daphnes, the Rosalinds, the Elliots were trained from childhood to look for every sign of wealth and to attach themselves to the people who had it. The Samanthas, the Bens, the Pace Dollarsons, were inculcated with an inner radar that resonated to the extra energy and sparkle that achievement and position throw off. The Myrons and Ames managed to keep themselves informed and did not hesitate to grab advantages that came their way.

Many of the people who don't consider themselves rich or well-connected simply don't pay much attention to who else has what or does what or knows whom, not in detail, not with the kind of thinking that is geared to useful connections. In fact, in a kind of sour grapes show of independence, some people scorn the rich kids at school, become standoffish about the rich neighbors, don't keep in touch with the rich relatives, and would never think of going out of their way to exchange a pleasant word at the office with someone who is known to have an independent income. When these scorners are also ambitious, the shunned rich colleagues, relatives, neighbors and classmates become overlooked resources. They are hidden connections that might be reestablished.

If you are aiming for upward mobility it is your responsibility to become aware of the people richer and better connected than you in any environment in which you find yourself. Start by identifying the richest person around and work down. Who is the richest person in your family? What is your relationship to this person? How old is he or she? What marital status? Do you know the current address and phone number? Dates of birth and anniversaries? When is the last time you were in touch with this person? When could you make the next opportunity to be in touch? How could this person's wealth or connections be most helpful to you? How could you make yourself of remarkable use to this person?

Who is the richest person where you work? Being even a little bit better off counts. Someone whose family has a summer house to visit or a car to borrow when you have none, counts as "richer." Someone who has a much larger apartment than yours, in which you could give a joint party, counts. Someone who has a skill or an interest from which you could learn or a connection from which you might benefit counts, too.

Who was the richest person in your class at school? When were you last in touch with that person? Why did you lose touch? Why wasn't that person a close friend? What did you like about that person? What flattering anecdotes and stories can you remember? What would it take to become friends with that person now?

Who is the richest person in your neighborhood? Or on your block or in your apartment building? If you have not met that person, what excuse could you come up with to strike up a conversation? What cause would you have to join? What petition might you circulate? In what bit of architectural or historical research could you enlist his or her aid? Which other neighbors would you have to get to know as a natural bridge? What would you have to look for, and offer, in order to pursue an acquaintance? How many people richer than yourself can you get to know in your immediate, daily environment?

Many people's social lives evolve from the people they meet because of their children. A single parent with limited access to other social life may have opportunities to meet people and develop a network through a child's school and extracurricular activities, through parents' organizations, through children's play dates and overnight visits, through volunteering for class outings and other school events.

The excuses for not developing the hidden connections go like this: they're snobbish; they're stingy; they're cliquish; I can't afford to keep up with them; I don't fit in; they'd be ashamed to have their friends meet me; they'd think I was pushy; they're terrible people; they'd turn me down; it's too much work; they're boring; they don't like anything I like; we never got along in the past; why would we now? I wouldn't have the nerve after all this time; I can never forgive them for what they said back then; I wouldn't know how to reach them. All the excuses add up to: I don't deserve to get what I want. Or the other side of the same coin: The world should lie down and die for me; I shouldn't have to do anything unpleasant or make any unusual efforts to accommodate myself to anyone else.

Rich people can be difficult. Some may be mean, selfish,

spiteful people. Some may be people who have worked with ferocious dedication and sacrifice to lift themselves out of the miserable circumstances and self-defeating attitudes of their early environments. Some struggle up from severe economic and emotional deprivation. Some have had to overcome prejudice that has operated very harshly, over long periods of time, against their ethnic group. Those who succeed often don't want to be dragged back down by old acquaintances and relatives unwilling or unable to make the same efforts and sacrifices.

In my own family there was a man who, for many decades, conducted one of the most famous orchestras in the country. The conductor's mother and my paternal grandmother were first cousins. Their sons had only one brief contact as young men. When the conductor's father came to New York to visit, my father took some time out from his beginning professional practice to show the older man around. The conductor expressed his appreciation by sending my father some tickets to the theater where he was leading the orchestra. My father, a taciturn and fastidious man who loved music, did not pursue any further contact with his distant cousin.

In later years, my father's sister and her husband attended one of the famous orchestra's concerts and went backstage afterward to introduce themselves. They were not serious music lovers or regular concert goers. Their manners were not polished. In fact, they were rather rude and insensitive people. They presented themselves to the conductor familiarly as the children of his mother's cousin. They were greeted with a stony absence of recognition. Cruel snobbery? Perhaps. Excessive protection of an image? Perhaps. But the couple were crude curiosity seekers, hoping for a little reflected glory. They offered nothing attractive or even safe to a distant relative of talent and discipline, living and working hard in a competitive and cultured environment that was not naturally sympathetic to his origins.

## *Tenacity*

So the excuses are sometimes the truth. Those rich relatives and the other hidden connections may not want to associate with a newly emerged striver unless they can see that he or she has something acceptable to offer. They are certainly not just sitting around, waiting to be discovered.

But they are not all necessarily going to close the door firmly and forever, the way the conductor did on his unappealing second cousins. Some rich relatives will welcome a "poor relation" who simply dresses right and speaks correctly and is courteous to their friends. They may even value a relation who has developed some knowledge in the areas that interest them, be they shopping, fly fishing, wooing board members, organic gardening, Montessori schools, or gossip about the financial worth of neighbors.

Rich old Aunt Sally in the Palm Springs or Miami Beach condominium may be lonely and love visitors. She may have friends who have unmarried children of just the right age and degree of prosperity. Those children come to visit, too. The residents of those communities get social points for displaying visiting children, grandchildren, nieces and nephews. So a visiting niece or nephew might meet someone else who is being displayed and, in the circumstances, is eager for a sympathetic connection. Or a phone number might be transmitted to an eligible someone back home, with a glowing recommendation.

Sometimes smart strategies backfire. There was middle-aged Mildred, who looked up her rich cousin Herman, or Horace, or Henry, her contemporary. He had never married. She was divorced. Something like a romantic relationship began to develop. Then, suddenly, he dumped her and married a twenty-six year old. She went off in a furious sulk and refused ever to speak to him again. She was entitled to her hurt and angry feelings, but she might have chosen behavior more advantageous to herself.

She might have sent a warm letter of congratulations and understanding. She might have made a short visit after the bride and groom had settled in. She might have been friendly to the bride and offered a modest, personal gift that showed approval. She might have developed the role of protective godmother to that marriage and become a frequent, welcome visitor. Herman, married, might entertain more. A lot of the couple's friends would be his age. Wouldn't the bride be delighted to steer the available men to Mildred? Of course if the marriage suddenly soured and ended, Mildred could be right there, as comfort and consolation prize for a sadder and wiser but (one hopes) not too much poorer, Herman. If the marriage continued, Mildred could have used her relationship with the couple to expand her opportunities and to enlist some allies in her search for the life and the man she wanted. Instead, she closed them off.

Old girlfriends and boyfriends are a frequently overlooked source of hidden connections. There is, of course, hurt pride and anger to be lived down. There is suspicion and jealousy on the part of the spouse. There is sometimes a dog-in-the-manger attitude on the part of the person who left. He didn't want his former love, but he doesn't really want anyone else to have her, either. Or he just wants to get away without being embarrassed or reminded of his guilt. Treating that person convincingly as a valued and admired friend whose choice was finally acceptable requires iron discipline and tact, but if he or she has single friends of the caliber the rejected lover is seeking, a "wise" and "mature" stance could be worth it.

It is possible to look up old school classmates, even if it takes joining an alumni committee, a fund-raising drive, a student recruitment campaign, or a reunion program, to do it. Sometimes all that's needed is a letter, an "I was reminded of the old homeroom roll call, and I wondered what happened to...?" Or, "I'm going to be travelling near your town next month, and I wondered if we could get together..." When old schoolmates do get together, picking up old threads can be awkward at first. The seeker must present himself or herself as reasonably contented and enjoying life, not as a beggar asking for refuge. He must look and listen very carefully to understand who these people are, what they care about, and what to offer them.

Perhaps their Jaguar is in the shop more than on the road. Jack Nimblestriver would probably know a wizard of a foreign car mechanic not too far from where the old school friends live. He doesn't think this information is extraordinary, but it endears him to the couple and helps a dormant connection blossom into an active friendship. If Jill Upperclimbing's old classmate's spouse is trying to track down literature on the design of eighteenth-century gardens, Jill would know that, just two blocks from her office, there is a store specializing in rare books on art and architecture.

Or the couple is coming to Jill's city for a conference. They will stay in a luxury hotel and go on a shopping and gourmet dining spree, but they have a hankering to see the bohemian side of life. Jill takes them out for a tour of the far-out art galleries, the funky clubs, the experimental theater up two flights of stairs behind a garage. They think she is clever and original, maybe even glamorous. They are happy to keep in touch, if she will continue to initiate most of their contacts. One day they call to tell her about a fascinating man, just divorced, who is being transferred to her city...

These particular examples will not suit everyone, but they may stimulate different imaginations with ideas appropriate to different individuals' resources. Readers seriously seeking to marry up will have to devise their own enticements out of the circumstances of their own lives and the needs of the people with whom they want to connect. It can't always be done. But often it can.

The more a candidate for marrying up practices thinking

this way, making mental connections, coming up with things to offer and exchange, the more likely it is that those old associations can be revived. If the determined mover-up has gathered sufficient information, understood the subjects correctly and been helpful or pleasing, the people with whom he or she reconnects—as well as those met for the first time— are more likely to arrange for meetings with other people they value. They are likely to be inclined, with gentle encouragement from the mover-up, to include him or her more frequently in their social lives.

# 10

## Appealing
## to the Privileged

### Visibility

It used to be said among the upper classes that a lady should be mentioned in the newspapers only three times: when she is born, when she marries, and when she dies. With some allowance for patriotic service in times of crisis, the same was true for a gentleman. Many aristocrats still prefer complete privacy for themselves. However, rootless American restlessness infects all classes enough for most aristocrats to be interested in *other* people who are mentioned in the news. Visibility can become a substitute for lineage, and it does not always have to be earned by exalted or unique achievement. Public attention for anything reasonably respectable can function as a kind of social endorsement.

What is not respectable cannot be rigidly defined, because standards change so frequently, but this category is likely, at the moment, to include such activities as mud wrestling, belly dancing, serving as a surrogate in sex therapy, petty embezzling and ballot box stuffing, exposing routine corruption and publicly teaching people how to marry money. Anything illegal or immoral done on a large enough scale and producing

big enough profits has a chance of becoming respectable eventually. There are ex-call girls gracing the drawing rooms of
stately mansions and the programs of venerable charity committees. There is one-time mob money financing top drawer
prep school educations and diplomatic service.

In the what-have-you-done-lately? social life of our more
competitive urban centers, any sort of visibility is likely to
expand one's social viability to some extent. Writing a book
about your rape or your cancer surgery, getting a signed
editorial in the newspaper, appearing on a TV talk show,
assuming the presidency of an organization, being identified
as the friend of an elusive celebrity, accepting a prestigious
appointment or getting fired from one, acknowledging a past
liaison with someone currently prominent, all are likely to
bring in a few dinner and cocktail invitations from new sources
and exposure to other people's networks.

Even potential visibility or the potential for giving others
respectable exposure, can provide social coinage. Let it be
known, vaguely, that you are working on free-lance jour-
nalistic assignments, and you will be invited to half the ambitious cocktail parties in town. Let it be known that you have
applied to nursing school, and your name will disappear from
those same invitation lists within six months.

## Aiming Correctly

Cal Bucksborn and Doug Middleworth drifted apart after
college, because each found it easier to slip into the patterns
natural to their finances and backgrounds. But if Doug and
Suzanne Middleworth had been determined climbers, they
would have been very attentive to the Bucksborns and their
priorities. Suzanne would have boned up on some of Bett's
interests, volunteered to work on a political committee and
produced needed signatures or benefit guests, become involved with the family service agency in her community and

called on Betts for policy guidance. A Suzanne reaches a Betts by listening to Betts, deferring to Betts' expertise, praising Betts' choices and adopting Betts' interests. She does not set out to change Betts' way of doing things. Doug would have taken up squash and played as a guest at Cal's club, covered for Cal when he almost got caught with a girl, flattered Cal by asking about production methods and recapitalization strategies. Different kinds of business opportunities, a social life based on purposeful advancement, and more influential future connections for the Middleworth children might have resulted.

Cal and Betts are from Old Money, Useful Money backgrounds. They take for granted the ability to have fine possessions and comfortable living arrangements, mix with distinguished people and provide themselves with convenient services. Praise for these things could offend them. They have to be commended for *their* opinions, *their* judgments, *their* wisdom, *their* effective functioning in the areas that interest them. Each privileged type operates within different value systems, and each has to be addressed differently.

A Barbara (who spends only where it shows and uses people as atmospheric props) is second generation New Money, aiming for the Statustocracy. She will want to be congratulated on snagging a congressman or a TV leading man or an artist who has been profiled in *Newsweek* for her big party. She will want to hear exclamations of delight that her patchwork dress is a Koos van den Aaker and her stencilled sheepskin coat is a Fendi. A Greg (innovative businessman with social flair) is a very much arrived Statustocrat from a No Money, Old Money background. He will want appreciation for the barbed criticism behind his jovial verbal parries with the senator at dinner and acknowledgment of his subtlety in choosing a champagne *nature* to point up the delicate tingle of the meringue glacée.

A Rosalind (the exquisite lint-picker married to her parents' choice), New Money on its way to becoming Useless Money if the portfolio holds up, would want to hear about the perfection with which she maintains her figure, how becoming the new little cluster of curls is just behind her ears, how expensive the new upholstery in her living room looks, and how adorably clever she has been in training Simon to give her a diamond of some kind for each anniversary. An Edith, the neglected, handicapped daughter of Old, Useful Money, would be happy to hear she has done almost anything well at all.

A Dan, self-made multimillionaire and prime specimen of flamboyant New, Slob Money, would expound, in the street slang of his childhood, his enthusiasm for the leukemia research lab he is funding and then, just before the butler can announce that lunch is served, insist that everyone pile into the car to go and inspect the lab site. He will require good-natured cooperation and enthusiastic response. A George (Francine's businessman husband), a more modest example of New, Slob Money, would enjoy the company of anyone who, over dinner at a moderately good restaurant, would allow him to talk at length about the competent way he handles things, the quick decisions he makes, the tact with which he deals with the family of a troublesome employee, and the coy surprise he arranged for his childrens' Christmas vacation. A Daphne, pure New, Snob Money, would want to include in her circle only someone who seems settled in a solid social or vocational position, unshakable in traditional ways of doing things, not likely to rock the boat with new thoughts or untried activities.

## Admiration

What applies to making friends applies even more to attracting and keeping suitors. The majority of people have very little tolerance for criticism or opposition. Even if they agree to accept critical judgments of themselves for the sake of a particular discipline, these are more of an ordeal to be endured in the interest of gaining certain eventual rewards. When people are rich or powerful and needed by others, there is seldom much reason for them to learn to develop more tolerance for criticism and differences of opinion. Conversely, most people never can get enough praise and admiration. A relationship can develop out of casual contacts simply because a determined suitor keeps finding things to appreciate about the person and telling him or her so.

"You do such wonderful things with a simple scarf." "You certainly have patience in explaining complicated processes." "You have the sweetest smile." "I love to go to meetings that you chair. You keep things moving along so well." "Would you help us select the gift? Your instincts about what suits people are so good." "I have never seen such agility on the tennis court." "How do you always manage to get right to the point?" "That flower arrangement comes from the palette of an angel." "You are what style is all about." "I will never forget the advice you gave me about alternatives." Coming up with a specific quote from that person, or referring to a past action, explaining how it helped you or why you remembered it, will make your praise and attention even more convincing. If the relationship becomes more intimate, the praise extends to its most intimate details.

Some people are suspicious of flattery and tend to dismiss it, but over a period of time, most people are more inclined to think well of someone who consistently and intelligently praises them than of someone who consistently criticizes or says nothing. It is important, of course, to base praise on something the speaker considers true. It usually is possible to find things to admire with conviction. The determined admirer is not deterred by the absence of immediate response or the fear of ridicule from observers.

To some extent the golden rule works when applied to

the exchange of positive feelings. Privileged people, like everyone else who has a choice, prefer to be around those who give the impression that they really are interested in them, like and admire them. A person in a relationship that could lead to marriage certainly is going to prefer a partner who consistently offers liking and admiration.

## Independence

Being liberal with praise and admiration, emphasizing the positive in one's dealings with another person, does not mean becoming a doormat. An individual's requirements, and the limits of the individual's tolerance, can be stated in a positive, charming way, backed up by a firm stand on having these limits and requirements respected. The potential partner is simply being informed that he or she is considered eminently willing and able to be pleasing, understanding and cooperative, and that the informant considers himself or herself entitled to be treated well. A doormat is a desperate person like Ames, someone who feels helpless and worthless. Abuse becomes the price of survival. As we saw in Chapter 4, the doormat will take anything rather than risk being discarded. The desperate doormat hanging on through endless humiliation is quite different from the generous, appealing, independent person who can tolerate some of another individual's flaws.

While people with money and power want cooperation and admiration, they also are attracted to a degree of independence. The balance can be tricky. First there has to be something about the candidate for marrying up that appeals to appropriate marital prospects. Then the candidate has to let the prospects know that he or she likes them and might be available to them. But the marrier-up who is too easily available probably will not be valued enough. So the matrimonial candidate has to demonstrate some willingness to accommodate the prospects, give them some taste of whatever wonderful attributes he or she has to offer, and then, without becoming cold or nasty, the candidate has to make it quite clear that he or she is not just hanging around waiting and hoping. While the prospects are definitely appreciated, and their company is found very enjoyable, the marital candidate is well able to continue life without them. If they believe that the candidate for marrying up really can survive comfortably without them, they might begin to believe that he or she is not interested only in their money. Rich people, like everyone else, want to feel that they are loved for themselves alone.

There is a scenario, with variations, that has been used successfully by many seductive, independent women and men. Perhaps a woman is being courted with intermittent enthusiasm by a rich man wary of personal commitment. At a time when he really seems to value her, she packs up, quite seriously preparing to move to another part of the world. At that point he may make up his mind and propose marriage. A man courting a rich woman who keeps him dangling among other suitors may, while remaining attentive to her, arrange to let it be known that he is being seen more often in the company of another woman with whom the first feels competitive. She may decide it is time to tag her property with a marriage license.

Sometimes the poorer person makes a display of not valuing the most obvious things the richer one has to offer. A woman courted by a diamond merchant finds jewelry unbecoming to her. If he is a fur broker, she has principles about endangered species. A man well qualified to step into a woman's family business emphasizes the opportunities and offers that attract him elsewhere. These are all risky games. The independent, poorer person really has to be willing and able to lose and to leave. It requires a competent, confident Samantha, not a floundering Ames. Sometimes this kind of self-sufficiency is won as a defense against early disappointments. The individual has learned to steel himself against ever needing another person more than that person needs him.

## Being Wanted

As we saw in Chapter 3, preferences in mates cannot be divided neatly into cultural or socioeconomic categories but are subject to the idiosyncracies of each individual's personality and past experience. If you are hoping to attract a rich husband through your delicate refinement and elegance, and the rich man you meet really wants a hearty earth mother to cradle his sweaty fears and respond to his dirty jokes with belly laughs, you are not likely to hit it off. If you can offer an aristocratic wife a perfectly tuned contender for the Olympic Gold Medal in sexual prowess, but the aristocratic woman you meet prizes only verbal subtlety and multiple listings in *Books in Print*, she is not likely to be impressed by you.

One of the most difficult tasks in life is to be objective about what one really has to offer and what other people value. To some degree, we all want to be loved just for ourselves alone, simply for being on this earth. If you can convince a potential spouse that this is the way you feel about him, you are way ahead. But don't expect him—or her—to do that for you. Ideally, we only get that sort of unconditional love from our mothers in the first three or four months of life. We also want to be loved for something that was highly valued in our environment: breathtaking beauty, an I.Q. of 140, a batting average of .1000, an exquisite poetic sensibility, gifted hands that can make anything work, shrewd managerial skills, a magnetically warm and engaging personality. Very often people get so caught up in wanting to be loved for what they don't have or for what they have that others don't value, that they completely overlook the attribute that makes them appealing to others.

Being unable to compete in areas that inspired popularity in childhood and youth may help an individual to develop other important qualities. Beautiful, sexy young women and handsome, bright strong men are the usual stereotypes of desirability, but they don't all wear so well. A plain, shy twenty-three year old, left out a lot on the flashy singles scene, may discover at thirty-seven that the successful men she meets (who aren't chasing twenty-three year olds) really are looking for the tender caretaker and efficient manager she knows how to be. The round-shouldered grind behind thick glasses was lonely in high school, when the girls were only interested in football stars, but at forty, as an adviser to several cabinets on international trade agreements, he is in constant demand among a string of achievement-hungry heiresses.

Francine—witty, successful, plain and middle class—wanted to be glamorous and extraordinary. While her style and verve had appeal, it was the limits to her sophistication, her links to the ordinary, that made her safe enough to be really desirable to George. Ames had a fantasy of success and fame in a world of talent and style. She married a man who already had achieved her ambitions. Wally recognized that Ames' flair for appearances made her compatible, but what really drew him to her was the self-hatred and lack of confidence behind her willing adaptability. He wanted someone he could totally control. While Ben, the brilliant architect from humble origins, thought he was getting encouragement for his talent and relief from economic pressure, his rich upper-class wife, Meg, unwittingly wanted a vehicle for expressing her own critical high standards in public. Crusading against the obstacles to Ben's ideas interested her. Actually helping him to get his work built did not.

Many successful women today complain that the men they meet are turned off by bright women. They resent having to "hide" their "real abilities" and "lie" in order to attract and keep a man. Sometimes they don't realize that there is limited enjoyment in being around someone who is perpetually tooting his or her own horn. If a woman is successful and valued at work, she might just be able to ease off in private life and use her brilliance to discover, acknowledge and encourage whatever is remarkable and likable in her lover. If he feels sufficiently valued, he may develop some capacity for tolerating her talent and success. Successful men could also, usually, learn to be more modest and attentive at home.

## Supply and Demand

Another hard lesson to learn is that after infancy, we never will get everything we need from another person. Even the most loving and wonderful spouse will not supply it all. This is equally true for men and for women. No matter how loyal and devoted a couple may be, how much they enjoy each other, how much they share, certain preoccupations are better confided in a friend, certain interests are more satisfactorily pursued separately, certain triumphs and complexities are most appreciated by colleagues, certain persistent anxieties are best understood by professional counselors.

Often what was fascinating as part of getting to know someone gets dull if presented in detail on a daily basis. The long haul of a continuing relationship has endearing comforts (along with irritations) that are different from the excitement and suspense of a tentative or impassioned beginning. Married sex is seldom as exciting as a new encounter. Some people find compensation in being able to count on its availability and on knowing what will work; some don't. The intricacies of another person's business or profession may lose their mysterious fascination when they are familiar and understood, and the person who wants to talk about it may need new audiences from time to time. One reason smart people in enduring marriages like to make new friends occasionally is to provide new audiences for each other and new stimuli for creative and sexual energies. The preference is usually that the sexual fantasies be expressed in action with the spouse. Swinging causes trouble.

## What Do They Really Want?

My first career, in my early twenties, was in the advertising business. As I began to have some noticeable success, I found that I also had acquired some responsibility for entertaining the female executives on a major account and, in the course of a work project, made a devoted friend of an internationally revered poet. As my salary began to show signs of catching up to my accomplishments, I began to think about moving from the tiny studio apartment with its pretty but makeshift furnishings that I had inhabited for the first four years out of college. I mentioned these thoughts to a colleague who happened to care a lot about what "looked right" and what was "in." She replied, "Yes, now that you're entertaining people like Carl Sandburg, you should have more elegant surroundings." She didn't understand that the famous poet, who dealt with internal essences, emotional images and the feelings of appreciation emanating from others, would have been happy perched on an orange crate in a tenement. It was the striving executives, caught up in external status symbols, like my colleague, who required the tangible signs of success.

In the service of expanding networks, the seeker of upward mobility needs to become aware of the values on which people base their judgments of others. Among confident Old Money and people who give priority to intellectual and esthetic values, a personable newcomer could be admired for living in an apartment that consists of one room containing nothing but a futon mattress, a wall of serious books or phonograph records with simple equipment for playing them, and, on a bare floor, a clear glass vase holding a single flower. Snob Money, New Money striving for tangible symbols of achievement, might be very uneasy about such a setting and dismiss the newcomer as poor and going nowhere. These people usually need more concrete evidence of position and affluence. They want to recognize the price tags and the labels or make sure of some higher authority's seal of approval.

One of the simplest ways to find out what people value is to ask them. The person determined to connect pays detailed, penetrating attention to each individual. Fruitful questions and bold offers can spring from that attention and establish ties that bind. A general idea of what others value offers only an opening for exploration. For a snug and accurate connection, it is important to keep on observing and questioning, tactfully, to find out *exactly* what they mean.

In James Thurber's fairy tale, "Many Moons," a young princess gets sick. Her father, the king, promises that she can have anything she wants if she will get well. The princess asks for the moon. The king summons his wisest counselors and asks them how he can obtain the moon for his daughter. Each counselor reports it is impossible and explains why. Each explanation depicts the moon as larger, farther away, and made of a more unwieldy substance, than the one before. The king becomes discouraged. Then the court jester decides to ask the princess to describe the moon. She tells him that, when she sees it from her bedroom window, it is slightly smaller than her thumbnail and is made of gold. The jester has the court goldsmith make a little gold disk strung on a chain and gives it to the princess to wear around her neck. She is delighted and recovers instantly.

The counselors failed because they did not stop to consider what the princess meant by the moon. The jester succeeded because he decided to find out just what the princess really did mean. The moon she described turned out to be very simple for him to obtain and give to her. If you assume in advance that you know what someone you meet means by intelligent, beautiful, sexy, talented, loving, devoted, rich, or any other quality he or she values, you may fail, too. If you take the trouble to find out exactly what the person means, you may find that, to your surprise, you can supply exactly what is wanted.

# 11

# Finding the Privileged Appealing

## Staying on Top

A man from a super-rich and high-powered family had opted out of that environment and settled into obscure scientific research in middle-class surroundings. He once brought a brilliant, but socially provincial, colleague along on a visit to his mother. She was chic and lively, still prominent and well-connected. The scientist noticed that his guest looked uncomfortable as his mother rambled on in a stream of first-name references to famous statesmen, financiers, industrialists, publishers and entertainment stars. "You'll have to forgive my mother," he said. "She isn't name-dropping. Those are the only people she knows."

The scientist grew up accustomed to Sunday lunches at which he and the other children were a silent but alert audience, ready to parry the occasional testing question, at a large table where "the only people she knows" measured their acumen against each other. So far as he knew, that kind of "en garde" lunch went with the tennis court and the swimming pool, the stable, the summers abroad, the butler, the cook, the chauffeur, the gardeners, the waitresses and maids. In college he was surprised to find that some of his friends did not enjoy being invited home with him for the weekend. They came from affluent families, too, but ones that lived out of the public eye. They were not put off by the luxuries but by the tension and challenge in the atmosphere. Before accepting an invitation, the son's best friend at college was likely to ask, with a wary expression, ready to refuse, "Any 'interesting' people coming this weekend?"

So often, we think of the "idle rich" and the "leisure class." They exist. There are people who do nothing but surround themselves with beauty and comfort and pleasure. These are the Useless Money rich. It is sometimes possible for one or two generations to live that way, or even three or four, if they keep to themselves and make sure that someone dependable is minding the money. But usually, with Useless Money, the fortunes dissipate, the booze and pills and racing cars take their toll, the families degenerate and fade away until no one is left but someone like the silly, made-up crone whose diamonds shake as she giggles at her fourth husband cracking loud jokes about the twelve million dollars he married her for.

Being rich and powerful and responsible, staying on top of the world, is hard work. Watch Maggie Matterer, the scientist's mother, and her daughters at a reception where there are many strangers and out-of-town guests. It is quite unlike your average, affluent strivers' cocktail buffet, where the hostess says, "Hi! This is John Fortunequest. That's Polly Megamind. The bar's over there. Have a good time." And you're on your own for the rest of the evening to connect or flounder, whatever you can manage. Maggie and her daughters introduce each guest to someone specific. They offer a little information about each person, and they stay there for a minute or two to make sure the conversation gets started. "Polly, this is John Fortunequest. We're so lucky to have captured him on one of his rare trips back from Geneva. John, Polly Megamind's essays don't turn up in your business magazines, but some of her students do." If the conversation doesn't take hold, Maggie will stay with the newcomer and steer him to someone else. She will ask questions about his trip, what his plans are for the next week, what he has been reading lately, until she finds something that suggests a connection with another person in the room.

Maggie and her daughters never sit down for a cozy chat with a close friend. That's for the phone, or lunch the next day. If an enchanting man tries to monopolize her time, she'll tell him he's wonderful and offer him a quiet drink tomorrow or lunch next week, and get on about the work of making sure that no one is neglected or stuck very long with a bore or goes home before having talked with at least one person who made the evening worthwhile. At the top of the socio-economic heap, a smoothly whirling social life is business. It's a full-time job to organize, manage and orchestrate, even with excellent help. (Someone has to train the help, too.) Lists are kept up to date. Thank-you notes go out promptly, as do Christmas cards, wedding presents, condolences and congratulations. Logistics are coordinated with an efficiency that many a bureaucrat would envy. Cars are sent to airports, delicacies to ailing friends, caterer's birthday cakes to children away at school. Menus are planned. Place cards are arranged. Rooms are refurbished. And time is spent on reading to keep up with people, ideas and events.

When Maggie and her family are confronted with new people, decisions are made quickly about which ones to include. The actress returning to Broadway, yes. The wife of the owner of the paper mill in Ohio, no. The president of a prestigious college, yes. The pediatrician from Fargo, North Dakota, no. Maggie Matterer is so pleasant in her remarks, the timbre of her voice so mellow, that only after the paper mill owner's wife has left does she realize that absolutely no effort was made to encourage further acquaintance. She doesn't even have Maggie's unlisted telephone number. If the college president turns out not to measure up, he will be treated like other leftovers, a kind of charity case, never exactly invited but dealt with politely if he turns up in town for a meeting or a funeral or requesting information not too sensitive to obtain easily.

Securing ties to the interesting and screening out the less than worthy, those who do not fit in one way or another with the main focus, are ongoing processes. Staying on top requires toughness, even if it is masked by velvet manners. Not all of those who start out ambitious want to spend their lives competing in such an arena.

## Fortunate Is Not Necessarily Nice

Self-made rich people, those who rise to the top of a financial or corporate heap through their own talents and efforts, often are rough and humorless. The heirs to wealth, while sometimes charming, are sometimes not nice at all to be around. They can be impulsive and demanding, accustomed to having their whims indulged, their inspirations humored, their preferences honored. The priority given to self or self-interest can be monolithic. And some of the rich are just plain crazy. Much of the certifiable madness that puts a poor person into the back wards of state hospitals or out on the streets under a blanket of tranquilizing medication goes unchecked in a rich person who lives with a margin for waste, the paid supportive and managerial buffers that money can buy, and influential connections to smooth things over when necessary.

The person at the top usually is sheltered by advisers and servants, the luxuries of office and secluded homes, the deference of subordinates. The habits acquired at work, of being catered to, having wishes met before they are expressed, of finger-snapping commands being obeyed, are often brought home and continued there. Women are no less susceptible than men to acquiring the overbearing habits that go with power won through tough, competitive achievement. Social custom usually has required that women who marry maintain some veneer of "feminine" gentleness at home, but often it is pretty thin.

In an ideal world both men and women would learn equally to be shrewd and sturdy commanders at the office and tender caretakers at home. However, ideals are wishes, useful as guidelines for a better future, but nothing for which to postpone a life in the present. While a fair balance in marriage is preferable, one person is likely to be better at making personal concessions than the other. Usually the one who has the most power out in the world makes the fewest concessions at home, but it does not always work that way. Most people can think of at least one gentle, charming man who has an important position and a mean, sharp manager of a wife. She serves an essential function in his life. All the unpleasant tasks that don't suit his image are delegated to her.

There are marriages in which each partner assumes some of the unpleasant tasks and unpopular roles with friends and family. There are marriages in which each partner's preferences are allowed some chance for indulgence and in which major decisions and interests are equally shared. There are marriages in which sex is a generally satisfactory and reciprocal pleasure. However, torturers and benevolent despots also still exist in today's marriages.

Sex and money still are bartered in society as well as in what used to be called the demimonde. The scion of millions with the diamond bracelet draped over his erect penis, saying "Come and get it," is not a fiction. The casting couch, the promotion of those who do "favors," is a reality. For some people sex is like a baby's pacifier. They must never be without it. After a while they don't even know that they really never can be satisfied, because there is a difference between the pacifier and the breast, and they have become accustomed to seeking only new and better pacifiers.

Sexual liberation has not automatically disposed of all the women known for their seductive charm, willing and versatile performers in the bedroom, whose ecstasy is faked and who, consciously or unconsciously, despise the rich husbands who can be so easily fooled. There are others who still are unable to do anything but lie tensely on their backs and wait for it all to be over, and no matter how much money and position they bring him, they can drive a sensitive husband to despair. There are multimillionaires who cannot bear to be embraced, because any touch at all would be too humiliating a reminder of a certain underdeveloped organ's preference for repose.

Money and privilege turn up in all shapes and sizes. Old, New, Useful, Useless, Slob, Snob. Nymphs and satyrs cavorting in sexual marathons or tight, celibate souls. Pounding out orders with gold-tooled cowboy boots on the table or slashing strong men to ribbons in an icy whisper. Stretch limo or customized Jeep. Walls of damask or stamped Masonite paneling. Poring over Teilhard de Chardin or *Playboy* centerfolds. In couturier gowns or English tailoring or the unisex drab of camping suppliers. Brewing herbal teas or swilling sour mash. Terrified of aspirin or mainlining cocaine.

Even when it is contradicted over and over again by the individuals one meets, there is an image of money that is hard to give up. The rich en masse seem taller, healthier, packed more vigorously into their clothes, standing up straighter. Their skin is clear and glowing. Their stride is brisk and self-assured. Their voices ring out with authority and clarity even when exquisitely modulated. There is something cold and final in their graciousness. Even with friends, their manner steers clear of the effusive sentimentality allowed to flourish in the middle classes. They are trained to keep themselves apart from others.

## Fair Trades

Unlike the Maggie Matterers, riding the crest of successive waves of movers and shakers, many rich people are accustomed to spending most of their time with people they "always" have known—at school, camp, clubs, summer houses, dancing class, coming out parties, and on into the brokerage houses and the boards of philanthropies. They really don't have much training in dealing with strangers. They are accustomed to a history of shared experiences. A nickname, an anniversary, a shorthand reference to an old incident, can evoke gales of laughter or a flood of news. There is always an inquiry about somebody's old grandmother or new nephew, some gossip about a cousin's fiancé or an associate's peccadillos. The conversation may not be scintillating but it doesn't take much to keep it going. A newly met outsider shares none of this familiar frame of reference with the person. The insider is not accustomed to asking questions beyond a basic few that could rule out the newcomer as totally unacceptable, and that information probably already has been dispensed by whoever did the introducing in the first place.

As the seeker, it is up to the newcomer to have developed the skills and exert the effort to make things lively. It is too easy simply to let the answer to each question close another door because the newcomer never has been interested in Scarlatti or archery or cotton futures or reclaiming the old seaport. The terse, cool way in which one is answered can fool the uninitiated into thinking that the subject is not a major passion of the person replying. It may not be. But he or she simply may have been taught that it is not polite or worth the effort to impose one's enthusiasms on those who are not interested. So it is up to the newcomer to supply the

enthusiastic response. "Whose recordings would you recommend?" "Where do you practice? How far away are the
targets? What are the bows made of? You must have strong
arms." "Do you have to be a good gambler or a smart farmer?
What exactly *are* futures?" "What a wonderful project! Is there
anything that someone chained to a desk all day can do to
help?"

If the privileged person you meet is attracted to you as
an outsider because he or she is ready for some new interests
or new ways of doing things, it will be up to you to make
suggestions and be the guide. Some rich people grow up
curiously jaded. Anything fascinating already has been done
superbly by someone they know. There seems to be nothing
outstanding left to master, no place to stake out a new claim,
no reason for enthusiasm. If you have unusual knowledge
or show signs of success in a brand new field, you may become desirable as an instrument for vicarious enthusiasm.
Or the privileged person may find it stimulating to introduce
familiar old treasures to your "new," interested eyes. It may
be invigorating to receive your fresh admiration for achievements the individual has taken for granted for years. These
could range from winning the Maclay trophy in equitation or
growing healthy delphiniums in a hot climate to putting together a conglomerate.

The richer person's manner may remain flat. If you continue to see each other, it may always be up to you to provide
the vitality. What he or she provides for you—personally
and emotionally or on a broader social scale—determines
whether or not it is a fair trade. If you continue with this
person you may have to give up old pleasures in order to
concentrate on the new things you are learning and are supposed to be enjoying.

You may have to give up comfortable old friends, because
there is no time to see them, they do not fit into your new
circle, and you have to concentrate on demonstrating that

you can get along in your potential mate's environment. You may have to learn to play bridge or golf, put live bait on a fish hook, wear skirts when you'd rather wear jeans or a tie when you'd rather wear a T-shirt, drink wine when you'd rather have a beer, freeze at a football stadium when you'd rather bask at a beach, dress up and sit through *Die Valkyrie* when you'd rather lie around watching sitcoms. A comfortable lover with whom you might have become serious if you had been less ambitious may form an attachment elsewhere before you know whether or not you really have a future with the new, more upscale person.

A notion that has not been very popular in recent decades is that in order to get something we want a great deal we may have to give up a few other things we also want. Only you can tell what it makes sense for you to give up and what is too great a sacrifice. It is possible to make a mistake, marry the rich person for "sensible" reasons and regret it later. Of course, marriages among economic equals, rushed into out of pure, heedless passion, often produce the same amount of regret. People make all kinds of sacrifices for careers, for homes, for children, for others whom they believe they love. Sacrificing immediate indulgence for long-term well-being may not turn out to be such a hardship at all.

## Beauty and the Beast

In seeking someone to marry, a lot more thought often goes into what's wrong with a person than into what's right. Human beings have a way of finding what they seek. If you are looking for flaws you'll find them. The virtues may go unnoticed. And a perfectly good potential spouse gets eliminated without ever really being known. Very often, what we like in another person is based on what we don't like in ourselves. We pick a mate to correct for our flaws, to use as a magic mirror in which we can see what we long for in ourselves. If she feels ugly, she wants him to be handsome so that she can feel beautiful. If he is shy and tongue-tied, he wants her to be outgoing and glib. If she feels helpless, she wants him to be powerful. Of course, we eventually may hate the mate who represents what we want to be, because we discover we have not been transformed through marriage.

It is the tale of Beauty and the Beast, from the beast's point of view. But we are secret beasts, imprisoned in our hideous and frightening flaws, seeking our version of the perfectly beautiful and virtuous maiden whose generous love will change us into magnificent princes. For a satisfactory life that could include a good marriage, we would do better to apply some energy consistently into transforming *ourselves*. Whether it is the way we look or walk or sound, our intellectual ignorance, our poor judgment, or fear of our own veiled emotions, a little steady work toward self-improvement can go a long way toward expanding our capacities for worthwhile relationships.

There is nothing wrong about spouses supplying opposites, features the other lacks, so long as there is a reasonable limit to each person's self-hatred and expectations of magical compensation through the mate. If he is dull, she provides the sparkle. If she is superficial, he provides the depth. If he is gloomy, she provides the optimism. If she is capricious, he supplies the common sense. If he is suspicious of everything, she supplies a rational amount of trust. If her moods swing wildly, he provides the even temper. If he is stingy, she is generous. If she is overly expansive, he furnishes the restraint. They function as a complementary team.

To make personal teamwork possible, it pays to find and to develop things to be proud of, things to like about oneself. When we come to terms with who we really are, and we respect that person, we often find ourselves more open, less critical and perfectionistic about the people who are available to us. Those for whom success is more than skin deep work at making the most of their own abilities; they develop curiosity and resilience in dealing with others; they make sure to find satisfaction in the lives they are living now. Instead of having to try to compensate for unworthiness through a magically endowed spouse, they are more likely to attract a spouse who is worthy of them, and they are more likely to recognize a worthwhile potential spouse when they meet one.

# 12

## The Best Way to Marry Up

### Entitlement

When I was twenty-two and supporting myself entirely on the sort of small-change paycheck a graduate of one of the Seven Sisters colleges considered herself lucky to earn in the 1950s, I found myself one afternoon on the expensive part of New York's Madison Avenue. In the window of a small shop, I saw a dress that looked as if it had been made for me. I suspected the shop was out of my price range. I feared a haughty reception. But I went in anyway and tried on the dress. Yes, it was "my" dress. And yes, the price was just a little more than two weeks' pay. I was mortified. I apologized. I had no right to try on the dress, to enter the store, to walk the earth. The saleswoman cheerfully disagreed. "Who knows?" she said. "We may not sell the dress this week. And next week a check may came in for you . . ." I knew no check could possibly come in next week, but I found her attitude comforting. She reminded me that pleasant wishes came true in certain lives. Apparently, I appeared to be within the range of those for whom such good fortune was possible. However, I was not yet convinced.

In his book, *The Privileged Ones,* the child psychiatrist Robert Coles describes the children of the rich as growing up with a sense of entitlement that makes them psychologically different from other children. They develop this sense from growing up in an environment in which there are always many opportunities for growth and satisfaction and in which wishes and fantasies often become realistic possibilities. Coles writes: "It so happens that among rich children one day's apparently fatuous, excessive fantasy or dream can turn into the next day's activity . . . "

One of the examples Coles gives is that of a mine owner's son who would like to see an airplane added to the family's already extensive options in equipment and travel, and within the year, the family acquires its own private airplane. "For those lucky, a sense of entitlement develops—the merger of what they have learned would be ideal and what they have actually experienced, into an ongoing attitude toward the world."

For those whose early circumstances have indicated a more limited range of realistic possibilities, a sense of entitlement often does not come naturally. It so happens that, three years after the dress shop incident, I became the owner of a second-hand, two-seater, single-engine airplane. I had had no serendipitous windfall. I still dressed in budget clothes. I traveled by bus to the airport where my plane was tied down. But my work had been rewarded with small but steady raises in pay. I had a credit rating. And my sense of entitlement had developed to the point where I could risk concentrating on what mattered to me most, even if other areas remained stringently restricted, and even if my choices seemed odd to others. At that time, flying airplanes was my passion. Owning one was a dream come true, assisted by a clear order of priorities and some sacrifices.

As I have suggested before, exploring one possibility often opens up others in unexpected directions. My personal in-

terest in aviation became valuable at work when the advertising agency acquired a major airline account. A year later I
was its top TV writer. No other woman even had been invited
to submit material for that account. The advertising job itself
had begun as a stopgap, to pay my way while looking for
more "creative" opportunities in the theater. In the course of
work on the airline account, my friendship with Carl Sandburg evolved. He introduced me to his widowed brother-in-
law, the renowned photographer, Edward Steichen. We fell
in love and, despite the logical contraindication of a vast
difference in ages, married within the year. All this came
about because I had felt entitled to pursue as fully as possible
a somewhat unusual interest in flying!

Flying airplanes had not been the first unusual venture
in my life. I had been active in civil rights and radical politics
as a high school student, twenty years before other middle-
class young people took them up *en masse*. I also taught horseback riding to children while my classmates cheered at football games. I worked in summer stock theaters for pay while
my college classmates were camp counselors or toured Europe. I took myself to polo games while my contemporaries
at the office schemed to attract dinner dates. But I also ignored
opportunities for building networks and did not follow
through on ambitious ideas beyond the first couple of rejections. Intimidated by the breezy conversational innuendoes,
I fled that chic Fifth Avenue cocktail party, the thank you for
working on the polo-connected benefit. Diana Barrymore,
star of a summer stock play in which I had a small role, sent
me to her agent, but when he told me to lose weight, I gave
up and did not go back. When the friend-of-a-friend producer
at Studio One returned my play script with the comment that
fantasy, no matter how talented, had no audience on TV, I
did not send it elsewhere.

Perhaps it was the timing, a point in my young life when
I was beginning to experience self-sufficiency and have some

small success and recognition on a job, but the refreshing comment of the saleswoman in the Madison Avenue dress shop had stayed in my mind as the mark of a turning point. It was a time when I finally began to consider myself someone for whom there might be possibilities, if I were determined enough to stay with them and flexible enough to shift directions when the possibilities shifted. It was a toehold on entitlement.

## False Claims and True Contenders

Some people, like my husband, grow up with a sense of entitlement without ever having had a great deal of money. They can get it from an environment in which certain money equivalents are open to children considered to have potential. Superior resource facilities, sensitive teachers, encouragement of abilities, scholarships and prizes, all can help. Other, more personal factors also contribute to its development.

Being, like my husband, the favorite child of a confident and not overindulgent mother is a good start. The mother communicates basic approval of the child, real pleasure that he exists. The mother lets him know that she believes he is entitled to the best the world has to offer, but since the world is the way it is, he will have to have some sensitivity to other people's needs, work hard, develop his abilities, use them well in order to take his rightful place. Basically, that child starts out in life feeling loved. Love provided successfully by the environment, another' person, or oneself, is the core of realistic entitlement. It is almost impossible to feel love for oneself without having first felt loved by somebody else. If it doesn't happen satisfactorily anywhere else in life, that experience often can be provided in the right kind of psychoanalysis.

In *The Privileged Ones*, Robert Coles distinguishes between realistic and narcissistic entitlement. When it is realistic, the child also develops a sense of responsibility, the obligation to prove himself through disciplined efforts and, often, to make a contribution to the world. What distinguishes him from the child who does not feel entitled is the belief that he can be successful in his efforts and that it will be possible to make some worthwhile contribution. I see entitlement as the stance of Useful Money applied with affection. It is not *Everything will come to me because I am rich*. Rather, it is *Because I am rich, I have had the advantage of excellent opportunities, and it is my responsibility to make the best use of them that I can*.

Narcissistic entitlement is a desperate illusion hopelessly pursued by those who have been severely deprived and those who have been extremely overindulged. Neither ever has felt really loved. They *must* have attention, recognition, money, nice clothes, beautiful surroundings, luxury objects, pampering services, sexual soothing and entertaining distractions. They require constant rewards and efforts from others, way out of proportion to the efforts they are able to sustain themselves. Whatever or whoever makes them feel good for the moment is highly valued. Whatever interferes with good feelings is scorned and discarded. They can be seduced into superficially attractive relationships in which they then are abused (like Ames). They actually may be brilliant, beautiful and talented, but they can't be counted on to perform well. Underneath they feel ugly, stupid, unlovable and worthless. Their endless, impossible demands are a hopeless attempt to escape their true feelings. The narcissist is not consumed with self-love but with the constant, futile effort to overcome self-hatred.

The narcissistically entitled may be appealing on first encounter. Often they glitter most enticingly, but just as often their charm wears thin as others realize that interest, care and generosity are a one-way street. Realistically entitled people tend to be attractive to others on a long-term basis. There is a sense of reciprocity and cooperation. They are not nec-

essarily undemanding, but their expectations are within reason. They are willing to accommodate another's needs but
will not tolerate someone who consistently takes advantage
and abuses them. They have no need to be cast as martyrs
or victims for the sake of procuring some sympathetic supplies. However, they can afford to expend some energy, make
some efforts that do not result in immediate rewards. They
may not glitter, but they are more likely to wear well.

Our attitudes and the impressions we make reflect the
presence or absence of the sense of realistic entitlement. If
you have it you are likely to create some of the following
impressions. You know the ropes. You are willing to learn
and to test your skills along the way. You are able to take
advantage of opportunities; you are not encumbered by false
modesty or defensive arrogance. You are resilient in the face
of obstacles. You will retain your values and your priorities,
without unnecessary rigidity, even if they are unpopular. You
are capable of discretion and of consideration for others' feelings.

## Winners and Losers

The students who found my *How to Marry Money* classes
helpful were most often those who were able to start thinking
realistically about where and with whom they fit in the world.

A successful woman in an unusual international career
realized she had been thinking only about what a man had
to offer her and not what she had to offer a man. She also
realized that, for her, marrying up meant marrying someone
whose achievement and sensibilities were simply equivalent
to her own and who would encourage her to continue in her
career. She had access to extremely wealthy men, but they
were lacking in the qualities that mattered to her most. She
began to explore and change the behavior patterns that had
kept her from responding to the kinds of men who really

interested her. Within a few months, a man startlingly close to her description of her ideal turned up and fell in love with her. It is not a Cinderella story. There were practical and emotional difficulties. There were disappointments. But they married. They loved each other. They were willing to learn to make it work. She reports that life is more complicated but it feels fuller and more deeply enjoyable.

A professional man had scorned the hometown pickings, called the upper-class women in his community narrow-minded and dull. He began to see that part of his attitude was a defense he used automatically to deal with the fact that his slight build and esthetic interests did not fit a certain macho stereotype. He was as worried about the disapproval of future male in-laws as about rebuff by a potential bride. He realized that his preoccupation with rejection had prevented him from spending any time identifying the qualities that he really valued in a woman. Once he came to terms with his own worth and became specific in his tastes, he could differentiate among the individuals in his community and apply very easily the principles of selective network building with matrimonial intent.

Some students, frightened of giving up familiar, unreal images or customary disappointments, did not fare so well. A beautiful young woman described her legitimate job with its potential for almost unlimited earnings and an excellent spin-off social life. The job required consistent hard work. She was popular and sporadically superb at her work, but despite this evidence of brains and personality, she insisted that she had nothing to offer in a personal relationship other than a rather passive body. She revealed that she made no effort to sustain relationships with any of the attractive and successful men she met. In fact, she resented making any efforts at all. She slacked off at work frequently; she had discovered she could make up the lost income with the help of certain not-so-appealing rich men who were willing to be helpful financially in return for minimal sexual favors. At first when she spoke, she asked fo help in combating her "laziness." She appeared to be looking for direction toward a constructive future. Eventually, as she rejected all suggestions quickly and firmly, it became clear that she was using this exposure to keep herself convinced that no effort could help, that there was no viable future for her, certainly none that included life with a man she could respect or enjoy.

The beautiful young woman was stuck in a rut worn early into her perception of life. She was dishonest in presenting her wishes for change but not consciously so. Neither were some of the other women and men conscious of dishonesty when they turned down every new idea, clung rigidly to past guidelines, and occasionally, with a kind of righteous chagrin bordering on relief, reported back with fresh failures just like ones they had had before. These students—a small minority in each class—were too angry or too discouraged to risk embarking on strange and difficult roads to new possibilities for improvement in life, through marriage or any other means.

## Something of Value

It is impossible to work seriously at the goal of marrying up without also working at improving one's life in a number of areas that are independent of marriage. It is entirely natural for people who have expanded their knowledge, upgraded their self-esteem, and improved their positions in the world to make friends and to marry at a higher social or economic level than the one from which they came. Their abilities, their interests, their attitudes and their frames of reference are often far from their starting places.

Being open to new possibilities and new ideas does not mean following someone else's recommendations precisely. To get along with various groups of people, we learn their standards and when to respect them, but the standards that matter most deeply are those we evolve for ourselves. Some-times an obviously desirable choice of mate turns out to be a disaster, while an apparently odd and incomprehensible choice is a realistically good one for the individual who makes it. My own marriage, to a man older than my parents, looked about as bizarre as a marriage could look, but my husband was—and remains a decade after his death—the best man I ever had met who made it clear that he really wanted me. I fell in love with his confident spirit, his talent, his apparent wisdom, his ageless, radiant vitality. It was not an easy mar-riage. Like all choices, this one closed off certain possibilities. But it opened up others. I am quite sure that I would not have done anything better with my life at that time.

Early in my marriage, at one of those dinner parties of movers and shakers, I was seated next to a man of celebrated brilliance. He had married into a bastion of wealth and influ-ence to which his abilities appeared to make him the rightful heir, and he had assumed the role with apparent grace. He and his wife appeared to be an ideal couple. But all of his remarks to me consisted of bumbling, dazed, speculative comments about how much money one must make in the advertising business (which I had left when I married). Bril-liant and daring as he was reputed to be, my dinner com-panion could not seem to imagine that an attractive young woman with a decent career actually could fall in love with a man so much older. Feeling badgered and insulted, I hated my questioner for his crude, mean spirit. We never met again. Some years later, in ways that insulted and damaged every-one around him, that man destroyed everything he had built up. I was not surprised.

Marriage does not have to be everyone's choice. Living in couples may turn out to be only a relatively primitive way station along the path of human development. For now, it remains the pattern most comfortable for most people. But no marriage is made in heaven. And none has to be made in

hell. Marriage is an agreement between two people. Often
it's a highly satisfactory agreement to disagree. In one of the
strongest marriages I know, a day seldom goes by without
at least one furious verbal exchange. These fights are like the
waving of banners proclaiming each partner's fierce individuality. Rather than threaten the marriage, they reinforce it.

All kinds of marriages are possible. What makes a marriage *good* is love. Money and influence are enormously helpful in all areas of life, and it is sensible enough to want to
have them. But life without love is bleak, no matter how we
disguise its absence with trinkets and distractions and dis-
plays of power. If money is an important part of your picture
of marrying up, there may be more ways available than you
think to combine money and love in marriage. One way is
to find someone to love who also has money. Another is to
marry someone you love and help that person to make money.
Still another is to marry someone you love and let that person
help you to make money.

Trite as it may sound, one of the best ways to get love is
to give it. The realistically entitled person, with so much to
offer, is the one who has felt loved. The narcissistically entitled person, with nothing to spare, has not. If you behave
in a loving way toward others, you will evoke whatever capacity they have for feeling love and for behaving in a loving
way toward you. If someone turns out to have no capacity
for responding with love, you don't have to hang around and
be a martyr. Martyrs usually are admired most when they
are dead.

The strategies I have described here for reaching out,
building networks, becoming informed and involved, finding
things to admire in people and ways to be useful to them,
are not entirely cold and ruthless manipulations. They can
be used that way. Many of the people mentioned here have
been more calculating than caring, more self-promoting than
sharing. (Maggie Matterer's son would not have had to flee

his natural environment for a middle-class disguise if it had offered more loving warmth and less glittering tension.) But these same strategies can be used with love even better than with just plain cold ambition. Love will make them much more enjoyable.

In a sense, any good marriage, any marriage in which the relationship itself brings satisfaction, is a form of marrying up. Each partner, by his or her presence and behavior, adds something of value to the other's life. What this book has attempted to explore is the very wide range of possibilities that, in a variety of circumstances, can be considered something of value.

# Index

361.49